CONTIGUOUS LINES

Issues and Ideas in the Music of the '60's and '70's

Edited by

Thomas DeLio

UNIVERSITY
PRESS OF
AMERICA

LANHAM • NEW YORK • LONDON

Library of Congress Cataloging in Publication Data
Main entry under title:

Contiguous lines.

1. Music—20th century—History and criticism.
I. DeLio, Thomas, 1951-   .
ML197.C753   1984   780'.904   84-19549
ISBN 0-8191-4329-4 (alk. paper)
ISBN 0-8191-4330-8 (pbk. : alk. paper)

All University Press of America books are produced on acid-free
paper which exceeds the minimum standards set by the National
Historical Publications and Records Commission.

for Kathy

Acknowledgements

The following materials have been reprinted by permission of their respective publishers and authors.

essays:

Robert Cogan, "Penetrating Ensembles," copyright © 1984, *A Sound Spectrum Picture Book*, Harvard University Press.

Thomas DeLio, "The Dialectics of Structure and Materials," copyright © 1980, *The Journal of Music Theory* (Spring, 1980).

_____, "Sound, Gesture and Symbol," copyright © 1982, *Interface* (Volume 10, Number 3).

Pozzi Escot, "Charm'd Magic Casements," copyright © 1982. Reprinted by permission of the author.

_____, "Non-Linearity as a Conceptualization in Music," copyright © 1981. Reprinted by permission of the author.

Alvin Lucier, "The Tools of My Trade," copyright © 1981. Reprinted by permission of the author.

Christian Wolff, "On Political Texts and New Music," copyright © 1983, *Literatur und Musik*, Erich Schmidt Verlag.

Wesley York, "Form and Process," copyright © 1981. Reprinted by permission of the author.

musical examples:

Robert Ashley, *in memoriam . . . Crazy Horse*, copyright © 1967, Robert Ashley. Reprinted by permission of the composer.

Pozzi Escot, *Neyrac Lux*, copyright © 1978, The Rocky Press.

Philip Glass, *Two Pages*, copyright © 1968, Dunvagen Music Publishers, Inc.

Christian Wolff, *Crazy Mad Love*, copyright © 1970, Christian Wolff. Reprinted by permission of the composer.

_____, *For 1, 2 or 3 People*, copyright © 1964, C. F. Peters Corporation.

Iannis Xenakis, *Nomos Alpha*, copyright © 1967, Boosey and Hawkes Publishers, Ltd.

miscellaneous:

Iannis   Xenakis,   *Formalized   Music*,   (pp.   226   -   227),
copyright © 1971, Indiana University Press.

Table of Contents

Introduction

One of the most striking aspects of the music of the 1960's and '70's was the extraordinary array of influences which issued from fields of endeavor traditionally quite foreign to the performing arts and which effected dramatic changes in compositional practice. Such diverse fields of inquiry as set theory, linguistics, anthropology and political science - to name but a few - have all had a profound impact on composers of this period. The eight essays contained in this volume all, in one way or another, reflect this tremendous diversity and, undoubtedly, will have a significant impact on any future evaluation of the music of these two decades.

This anthology is divided into two parts. The first consists of four essays of a highly technical nature, each author having formulated a detailed analysis of one particular piece by an outstanding contemporary composer. These four papers were chosen not only for their quality, but also because they reflect the broad spectrum of compositional approaches currently in vogue throughout Europe and America. Two contrasting European composers - Iannis Xenakis and Gyorgy Ligeti - and two contrasting Americans - Milton Babbitt and Philip Glass - were selected. Of course, the work of only four composers could never adequately represent the true richness and diversity of musical activity on two continents. It is hoped, however, that some sense of the breadth of current compositional practice will be conveyed.

Iannis Xenakis was born in 1922 in Rumania. His combined skills in mathematics, music and architecture have led to a distinguished career as an innovator in each of these three areas. His primary studies in musical composition took place in Paris under the guidance of Arthur Honegger, Darius Milhaud and Olivier Messiaen. As an architect, he worked with Le

Corbusier, with whom he collaborated on several projects. This author's report on Xenakis' remarkable work for solo cello, *Nomos Alpha* (1965), reveals a structure of extraordinary dimensions. Commissioned by Radio Bremen for cellist Siegfried Palm, *Nomos Alpha*, was written in homage to three great mathematicians: Aristoxenus of Tarentum, scholar and musician; Evariste Galois, the originator of the theory of groups; and Felix Klein, one of Galois' renowned successors. Expanding upon Xenakis' own writings on this subject, the author identifies two complementary creative impulses at work within the composition. The first generates a structure derived from mathematical group theory, while the second emanates less from any mathematical system than from the composer's direct manipulation of his sonic materials. The form of this work arises from the interaction between these two radically different methodologies, an interaction which raises issues central to any exploration of the origins of structure.

Gyorgy Ligeti was born in 1923 in Transylvania. He studied musical composition with Ferenc Farkas and Sandor Veress at the Budapest Acadamy of Music where he later taught harmony, counterpoint and analysis. He has also taught at the Darmstadt Courses for New Music, the Stockholm Music Acadamy and Stanford University. Since 1973, he has been a Professor of Composition at the Hamburg Acadamy of Music. Today, he is one of the most widely respected figures among the European avant-garde.

In the late '60's Ligeti composed two etudes for organ: *Harmonies* (1967) and *Colors* (1969). *Harmonies* traces the slow, almost imperceptible transformation of a single sonic event. In her penetrating analysis, Pozzi Escot reveals hitherto unexplored facets of this great work. In addition, she proposes a new method of analysis based upon the music's "hidden geometry," an aspect of musical structure which, until

xii

quite recently, also has remained relatively unexplored and which, as the author demonstrates, holds great promise in facilitating comparative studies among the music of various historical periods as well as between music and the visual arts.

Milton Babbitt was born in Philadelphia, Pennsylvania in 1916 and raised in Jackson, Mississippi. He received a BA from New York University and an MA from Princeton where he studied with Roger Sessions and is, at present, the Conant Professor of Music. He has taught at The Salzburg Seminar in American Studies, The Berkshire Music Center and The Darmstadt Summer Courses in Germany. Renowned as both a composer and theorist, his work has earned him membership in the National Institute of Arts and Letters and several awards from the New York Music Critics Circle.

Ensembles for Synthesizer was composed in 1967 at the Columbia-Princeton Electronic Music Center of which Babbitt is co-director. It it, he applies the principles of serial composition to a variety of sonic parameters including pitch, rhythm, register, texture and timbre. Robert Cogan's discussion of this piece is remarkable in several respects. It represents one of the first successful attempts to deal analytically with electronic music, a medium which evolved into a major art form in the '60's and '70's. It also represents one of the first serious attempts to develop a viable method of tone color analysis. As such, Cogan's paper is fraught with implications which far exceed its immediate purpose.

The American composer Philip Glass was born in Baltimore, Maryland in 1937 and studied at the Peabody Conservatory of Music, The University of Chicago and The Juilliard School of Music. In addition, he travelled to India on several occasions where he studied with Ravi Shankar. Since that time, largely as a result of his enormous success in revitalizing contemporary opera, he has come to be recognized as one of the most original figures in recent American music. *Two Pages* (1968) is one of the earliest examples of the repetitive style of composition with which Glass has come to be associated. As with all of his music this work is remarkable in its complete identification of content with process. In his paper, Wesley York introduces several new analytical techniques developed specifically to deal with Glass' work. These allow him to accurately delineate the most important features of this unique composer's style.

The second half of this book consists of four articles devoted to topics of more general interest such as notation, politics and technology. In the paper "Sound, Gesture and Symbol" this author considers recent developments in musical notation and demonstrates that changes in notation reflect new attitudes toward the creative process itself. Two such attitudes are identified and explored. The first concerns various relationships between the structure of an artwork and patterns of human behavior. The second deals with the notion of pluralism as exemplified in several types of "open form" compositions.

Pozzi Escot's article, "Non-Linearity as a Conceptualization in Music", outlines one of the crucial and pervasive elements of recent music. Non-linearity is a metaphor for discontinuity. It describes a condition in which the elements of a formal scheme are contiguous but not necessarily interdependent. As the author demonstrates, non-linearity is a concept which has influenced much European and American music since the turn-of-the-century as well as the music of many non-European cultures. More than that of any other period, however, the music of the '60's and '70's was characterized by this principle of non-linearity. Thus, while the most lengthy example in the paper happens to be drawn from the music of the early twentieth century, it was still included in this collection.

Alvin Lucier is one of the most remarkable and original American composers of his generation. His article, "The Tools of My Trade", is a simple yet thorough account of his evolution as a composer and documents the profound influences which recent developments in the sciences and technology have had upon his thinking and the structure of his music. In this essay he documents his work with such phenomena as brain waves and standing waves, and, in one instance, relates how his study of the echolocation techniques of bats inspired one of his most famous creations, *Vespers*. Throughout his discussion, the author identifies new discoveries in science and developments in technology which have had a tremendous impact on his compositions.

For the past decade another American composer, Christian Wolff, has been concerned with very different issues, in particular the association of certain progressive political ideas with his own rather unique concept of indeterminacy. Together with such composers as Luigi Nono in Italy and Cornelius Cardew in England, he has struggled to identify his music with a political position known as democratic socialism. As the title of his essay suggests, "On Political Texts and New Music" documents Wolff's own use of explicitly political texts in achieving his goals. The major work discussed is the cantata *Wobbly Music*, a setting for chorus and chamber ensemble of texts related to the history and ideals of the I.W.W. (The Industrial Workers of the World), an organization of tremendous importance to the American labor movement. This composition is a striking example of the depth to which political views can influence the creative process.

As may be gleaned from the breadth of ideas embodied in the eight essays outlined above, the '60's and '70's witnessed a tremendous diversification of compositional procedures. As theorists and historians begin to grapple with questions raised by this music, it is hoped that the contents of this volume will serve as both guide and catalyst for further inquiry.

Thomas DeLio
1982
College Park, Md.

Part One

The Dialectics of Structure and Materials

Thomas DeLio

Nomos Alpha is a work for solo cello written in 1965 by the Greek composer Iannis Xenakis. In it, Xenakis juxtaposes two radically different types of structure, producing a fascinating discourse on the relationship of the materials by which a structure is engendered to that structure itself. This paper will first present an analysis of the composition and, then, consider this one significant issue which arises from that analysis. Certain aspects of this discussion are borrowed from the composer's own analysis of the piece, which is summarized and considerably extended here.[1]

Nomos Alpha is in twenty-four sections which are separated into two layers of structure, here labeled levels I and II. Level I consists of sections 1 (mm. 1 - 15), 2 (mm. 16 - 30), 3 (mm. 31 - 45), 5 (mm. 65 - 79), 6 (mm. 80 - 95), 7 (mm. 96 - 111), 9 (mm. 126 - 142), 10 (mm. 143 - 160), 11 (mm. 161 - 177), 13 (mm. 188 - 202), 14 (mm. 203 - 218), 15 (mm. 219 - 234), 17 (mm. 249 - 264), 18 (mm. 265 - 280), 19 (mm. 281 - 297), 21 (mm. 317 - 332), 22 (mm. 333 - 350), 23 (mm. 351 - 364). Level II consists of every fourth section: 4 (mm. 46 - 64), 8 (mm. 112 - 125), 12 (mm. 178 - 187), 16 (mm. 235 - 248), 20 (mm. 298 - 316), 24 (mm. 365 - 386).

Level I

This structural level was fashioned with the aid of that branch of mathematics known as group theory. As such, before

3

moving on to the actual analysis, a few basic notions from group theory will be explained. A mathematical group is, first of all, a collection of elements over which a single binary operation is defined. A binary operation is one which operates on only two elements at a time. In addition, a group must exhibit the following properties:

    a) it is closed under the operation

    b) it is associative

    c) it contains an identity element

    d) it contains an inverse for each element.

For example the set of integers and the binary operation addition constitute a group structure. As such, they satisfy the four group properties:

    a) the set of integers is closed under addition: any integer added to any other integer always yields some integer

    b) it is associative: $(x + y) + z = x + (y + z)$, for any integer x, y and z

    c) it has an identity element: some element - in this case 0 - which when added to any other element, yields that other element; thus, $x + 0 = x$, for every integer x

    d) every element has an inverse: for any element in the collection there is another which, when combined with the first under the given operation, yields the identity element; clearly, every integer (x) has an inverse $(-x)$ under addition: $(2) + (-2) = 0$.

    The particular group structure which Xenakis employs is that group of twenty-four elements known as the octahedral group, so called because of its relationship to the structure of the polyhedron with eight sides (see Appendix). The elements

4

through which this group is expressed in Xenakis' music are permutations. The binary operation is composition (notated o).

The particular set of twenty-four permutations employed is listed below:

I	12345678	Q1	78653421
A	21436587	Q2	76583214
B	34127856	Q3	86754231
C	43218765	Q4	67852341
D	23146758	Q5	68572413
D2	31247568	Q6	65782134
E	24316875	Q7	87564312
E2	41328576	Q8	75863142
G	32417685	Q9	58761432
G2	42138657	Q10	57681324
L	13425786	Q11	85674123
L2	14235867	Q12	56871243

The logic guiding the specific labeling system used here will become clear as the analysis proceeds. For now, it should be observed that each group element is represented by a permutation of eight numbers.

It is especially useful for those unfamiliar with this branch of mathematics to think of the notation employed above as a form of shorthand. For example

$$A = 2 \ 1 \ 4 \ 3 \ 6 \ 5 \ 8 \ 7$$

is an abbreviation for

$$A = \begin{matrix} 1 & 2 & 3 & 4 & 5 & 6 & 7 & 8 \\ 2 & 1 & 4 & 3 & 6 & 5 & 8 & 7 \end{matrix}$$

Similarly,

$$D = 2 \ 3 \ 1 \ 4 \ 6 \ 7 \ 5 \ 8$$

is an abbreviation for

$$D = \begin{matrix} 1 & 2 & 3 & 4 & 5 & 6 & 7 & 8 \\ 2 & 3 & 1 & 4 & 6 & 7 & 5 & 8 \end{matrix}$$

5

and, of course,

$$I = 1 \quad 2 \quad 3 \quad 4 \quad 5 \quad 6 \quad 7 \quad 8$$

is an abbreviation for

$$
I = \begin{array}{cccccccc}
1 & 2 & 3 & 4 & 5 & 6 & 7 & 8 \\
\downarrow & \downarrow & \downarrow & \downarrow & \downarrow & \downarrow & \downarrow & \downarrow \\
1 & 2 & 3 & 4 & 5 & 6 & 7 & 8
\end{array}
$$

Thus, one should think of these twenty-four group elements as twenty-four permutation schemes represented, diagrammatically, by sequences of arrows similar to those shown above. The twenty-four group elements are, then, twenty-four distinct ways of permuting.

The operation o is defined as follows. As an example, one might take the binary operation A o D. A o D represents two interrelated stages in which the second permutation, D, is applied to the result of the first.

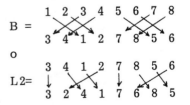

The result is permutation 14235867, which is equivalent to the group element L2. Thus, it may be said that A o D = 12. Similarly, B o L2 =

The result is permutation 32417685, which, of course, is

equivalent to group element G. Thus, B o L2 = G.

The complete range of compositions available within the group is summarized in the chart on the following page, which contains the results of compositions of all possible pairs. Chart A, known as an operation table, is read in the following manner. The result of operation A o D is calculated by finding the intersection of column A and row D.

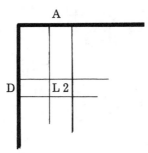

Next, for the purposes of the analysis which is to follow, several facts should be noted. Obviously, the identity element is I (12345678) since I is that permutation which leaves each of the eight numbers unchanged. Thus, when composed with any other element, the element I leaves that other element unchanged. In addition, the following elements are inverses: D and D2, E and E2 G and G2, L and L2. As such D o D2 = I, E o E2 = I, G o G2 = I, L o L2 = I; a fact which the reader can easily verify for himself.

Moving beyond the basic structure of the group itself, attention must be turned to a few simple aspects of its decomposition. First, the notion of a subgroup will be explored. A subgroup is a group which is contained within another group. For example, the subset of even integers, taken from the complete collection of all integers, itself forms a group under addition. The set of even integers is closed under addition and, together with that operation, exhibits all other group properties.

7

Chart A

↓	I	A	B	C	D	D^2	E	E^2	G	G^2	L	L^2	Q_1	Q_2	Q_3	Q_4	Q_5	Q_6	Q_7	Q_8	Q_9	Q_{10}	Q_{11}	Q_{12}
I	I	A	B	C	D	D^2	E	E^2	G	G^2	L	L^2	Q_1	Q_2	Q_3	Q_4	Q_5	Q_6	Q_7	Q_8	Q_9	Q_{10}	Q_{11}	Q_{12}
A	A	I	C	B	G	L	G^2	L^2	D	E	D^2	E^2	Q_7	Q_4	Q_5	Q_2	Q_3	Q_{12}	Q_1	Q_{10}	Q_{11}	Q_8	Q_9	Q_6
B	B	C	I	A	L^2	E	D^2	G	E^2	L	G^2	D	Q_6	Q_9	Q_8	Q_{11}	Q_{10}	Q_1	Q_{12}	Q_3	Q_2	Q_5	Q_4	Q_7
C	C	B	A	I	E^2	G^2	L	D	L^2	D^2	E	G	Q_{12}	Q_{11}	Q_{10}	Q_9	Q_8	Q_7	Q_6	Q_5	Q_4	Q_3	Q_2	Q_1
D	D	L^2	E^2	G	D^2	I	C	L	E	A	B	G^2	Q_3	Q_6	Q_4	Q_1	Q_{11}	Q_{10}	Q_8	Q_9	Q_7	Q_2	Q_{12}	Q_5
D^2	D^2	G^2	L	E	I	D	G	B	C	L^2	E^2	A	Q_4	Q_{10}	Q_1	Q_3	Q_{12}	Q_2	Q_9	Q_7	Q_8	Q_6	Q_5	Q_4
E	E	L	G^2	D^2	B	L^2	E^2	I	A	D	G	C	Q_{11}	Q_8	Q_6	Q_8	Q_7	Q_9	Q_2	Q_{12}	Q_3	Q_1	Q_{10}	Q_4
E^2	E^2	G	D	L^2	G^2	C	I	E	L	B	A	D^2	Q_{10}	Q_7	Q_9	Q_{12}	Q_2	Q_3	Q_5	Q_1	Q_6	Q_{11}	Q_4	Q_8
G	G	E^2	L^2	D	L	A	B	D^2	G^2	I	C	E	Q_5	Q_2	Q_1	Q_7	Q_9	Q_8	Q_{10}	Q_{11}	Q_1	Q_4	Q_6	Q_3
G^2	G^2	D^2	E	L	C	E^2	L^2	A	I	G	D	B	Q_9	Q_3	Q_{12}	Q_{10}	Q_1	Q_{11}	Q_4	Q_6	Q_5	Q_7	Q_8	Q_2
L	L	E	D^2	G^2	A	G	D	C	B	E^2	L^2	I	Q_2	Q_8	Q_7	Q_5	Q_6	Q_4	Q_{11}	Q_1	Q_{10}	Q_{12}	Q_3	Q_9
L^2	L^2	D	G	E^2	E	B	A	G^2	D^2	C	I	L	Q_8	Q_1	Q_{11}	Q_6	Q_4	Q_5	Q_3	Q_2	Q_{12}	Q_9	Q_7	Q_{10}
Q_1	Q_1	Q_7	Q_6	Q_{12}	Q_9	Q_5	Q_8	Q_2	Q_{11}	Q_{10}	Q_3	Q_4	A	L^2	D^2	E^2	L	B	I	G^2	G	E	D	C
Q_2	Q_2	Q_{11}	Q_1	Q_9	Q_4	Q_{10}	Q_6	Q_1	Q_8	Q_3	Q_{12}	Q_7	E	I	G	C	L^2	D^2	L	E^2	B	D	A	G^2
Q_3	Q_3	Q_8	Q_5	Q_{10}	Q_7	Q_{11}	Q_9	Q_6	Q_{12}	Q_2	Q_4	Q_1	L^2	G^2	I	L	B	E^2	D	A	E	C	D^2	G
Q_4	Q_4	Q_9	Q_{11}	Q_2	Q_8	Q_{12}	Q_3	Q_{10}	Q_5	Q_6	Q_1	Q_3	G^2	A	D	B	E^2	L	D^2	L^2	C	G	I	E
Q_5	Q_5	Q_{10}	Q_3	Q_8	Q_1	Q_9	Q_{11}	Q_7	Q_6	Q_4	Q_2	Q_{12}	E^2	E	A	D^2	C	L^2	G	I	G^2	B	L	D
Q_6	Q_6	Q_2	Q_7	Q_1	Q_2	Q_{10}	Q_3	Q_9	Q_4	Q_5	Q_8	Q_{11}	C	D	E	G	G^2	I	B	L	E^2	D^2	L^2	A
Q_7	Q_7	Q_1	Q_6	Q_{12}	Q_{11}	Q_3	Q_{10}	Q_4	Q_9	Q_8	Q_5	Q_2	I	E^2	L	L^2	D^2	C	A	E	D	G^2	G	B
Q_8	Q_8	Q_3	Q_{10}	Q_5	Q_{12}	Q_4	Q_2	Q_1	Q_7	Q_9	Q_{11}	Q_6	D	L	B	G^2	I	G	L^2	C	D^2	A	E	E^2
Q_9	Q_9	Q_4	Q_2	Q_1	Q_5	Q_1	Q_6	Q_3	Q_8	Q_7	Q_{12}	Q_{10}	D^2	B	E^2	A	D	E	G^2	G	I	L^2	C	L
Q_{10}	Q_{10}	Q_5	Q_8	Q_3	Q_6	Q_2	Q_4	Q_{12}	Q_1	Q_{11}	Q_9	Q_7	G	D^2	C	E	A	D	E^2	B	L	I	G^2	L^2
Q_{11}	Q_{11}	Q_{12}	Q_2	Q_4	Q_9	Q_8	Q_7	Q_{12}	Q_5	Q_{10}	Q_1	Q_6	L	C	L^2	I	G	G^2	E	D	A	E^2	B	D^2
Q_{12}	Q_{12}	Q_6	Q_1	Q_7	Q_4	Q_8	Q_5	Q_{11}	Q_2	Q_3	Q_{10}	Q_9	B	G	G^2	D	E	A	C	D^2	L^2	L	E^2	I

Clearly, the group of even integers under addition is contained within the group of all integers under addition and, as such, constitutes a subgroup of that group.

With respect to the group employed by Xenakis, one should note the following two subgroups which it contains:

subgroup 1 = (I,A,B,C,D,D2,E,E2,G,G2,L,L2)

subgroup 2 = (I,A,B,C)

Each of these collections forms a group under o.

Next the question arises as to the relationship of the remaining elements of the group to each of these subgroups. If one re-labels subgroup 1 as U1 and the remaining twelve elements as U2, the following operation table may be constructed (once again, the operation is o):

Chart B

	U1	U2
U1	U1	U2
U2	U1	U2

What is revealed by Chart B is that any element from U1 composed with any element from U2 yields some element from U2 (U1 o U2 = U2). Similarly, any element from U2 composed with itself or any other from U2 yields some element from U1 (U2 o U2 = U1).

With respect to subgroup 2, a similar operation table may be constructed. Here, however, the original set of twenty-four elements are partitioned into the following six non-intersecting sets:

$$V1 = \{I,A,B,C\}$$
$$V2 = \{D,E2,G,L2\}$$
$$V3 = \{D2,E,G2,L\}$$
$$V4 = \{Q1,Q6,Q7,Q12\}$$

9

$$V5 = \{Q3,Q5,Q8,Q10\}$$
$$V6 = \{Q2,Q4,Q9,Q11\}$$

With these six sets the following operation table may be constructed (as before, the operation is o):

Chart C

	V1	V2	V3	V4	V5	V6
V1	V1	V2	V3	V4	V5	V6
V2	V2	V3	V1	V5	V6	V4
V3	V3	V1	V5	V6	V4	V5
V4	V4	V6	V5	V1	V3	V2
V5	V5	V4	V6	V2	V1	V3
V6	V6	V5	V4	V3	V2	V1

What is revealed through this chart is that any element from V3 composed with any from V4 yields some element from V5 (V3 o V4 = V5). Similarly, any element from V5 composed with any from V2 yields some element from V6 (V5 o V2 = V6); and so forth. Unfortunately, space does not permit detailed discussion of just how these sets were derived.[2] For the purposes of this discussion, suffice it to say that they afford a somewhat simpler, more compact view of the original group structure. In a sense, they summarize certain relationships found in that original structure.

Having completed this brief survey of mathematical groups, the analysis may begin. First, with the help of Charts B and C, two paths through the group are determined. Xenakis chooses two elements with which to begin and orders them. Let us say that Q1 and Q9 will be the first and second elements, respectively. He first composes Q1 with Q9 , the result of which is D2 (Q1 o Q9 = D2). He then composes Q9 with D2, the result of which is Q8 (Q9 o D2 = Q8). Continuing, he composes D2 with Q8; and so forth. This motion is reminiscent of that used in

10

generating a Fibonacci series in that each succeeding element is fashioned from its two immediate predecessors.

With respect to the six sets associated with subgroup 2 the following thirty-six paths are possible:

V1 o V1...	V2 o V1...		V6 o V1...
V1 o V2...	V2 o V2...		V6 o V2...
V1 o V3...	V2 o V3...		V6 o V3...
V1 o V4...	V2 o V4...	.....	V6 o V4...
V1 o V5...	V2 o V5...		V6 o V5...
V1 o V6...	V2 o V6...		V6 o V6...

Each of these thirty-six paths is cyclic. For example:

V2 o V4 o V6 o V3 o V5 o V6 o (V2 o V4...

Of these thirty-six possibilities the composer chooses two:

V2 o V4 o V6 o V3 o V5 o V6 = Path V2 o V4

and

V2 o V5 o V4 o V3 o V6 o V4 = Path V2 o V5

Since each element Vi contains four elements from the original group, further refinements in these two paths are necessary. Path V2 o V4 may be expressed in sixteen possible ways:

$$V2 = \{D, E2, G, L2\}$$
$$V4 = \{Q12, Q7, Q1, Q6\}$$

D o V4 = DoQ12, DoQ7, DoQ1, DoQ6
E2 o V4 = E2oQ12, E2oQ7, E2oQ1, E2oQ6
G o V4 = GoQ12, GoQ7, GoQ1, GoQ6
L2 o V4 = L2oQ12, L2oQ7, L2oQ1, L2oQ6

All sixteen are, of course, cyclic, though they generate only eight different cycles, four of length eighteen and four of length

11

six

The four longer cycles are:

D Q12 Q4 E Q8 Q2 E2 Q7 Q4 D2 Q3 Q4 L2 Q7 Q2 L Q8 Q11

D Q7 Q11 E Q10 Q4 G Q7 Q9 G2 Q5 Q4 E2 Q12 Q11 D2 Q5 Q9

D Q1 Q9 D2 Q8 Q4 L2 Q6 Q11 G2 Q8 Q9 G Q1 Q11 L Q3 Q4

E2 Q1 Q2 E Q5 Q11 L Q6 Q4 G Q5 Q9 G2 Q7 Q4 L2 Q3 Q11

The four shorter cycles are:

D Q6 Q2 D2 Q10 Q2

E2 Q6 Q3 E Q9 Q3

G Q12 Q3 G2 Q2 Q3

L2 Q12 Q10 L Q9 Q10

The sixteen original paths reduce to only eight, since each of the four longer cycles can be generated from three of the sixteen pairs listed on the previous page. For example, the first of the longer cycles can be generated from D o Q12, E2 o Q7 or L2 o Q7:

D Q12 Q4 E Q8 Q2 E2 Q7 Q4 D2 Q3 Q4 L2 Q7 Q2 L Q8 Q11

Similarly, Path V2 o V5 generates sixteen paths of which only eight are different - four long and four short.

From these possibilities the composer chooses the following: for Path V2 o V4, D Q12 Q4...; and, for Path V2 o V5, D Q3 Q7... These are both paths of length eighteen and are presented simultaneously, over the course of the piece, and in one-to-one correspondence:

D Q12 Q4 E Q8 Q2 E2 Q7 Q4 D2 Q3 Q11 L2 Q7 Q2 L Q8 Q11

D Q3 Q7 L Q11 Q6 L2 Q5 Q7 D2 Q9 Q1 G Q5 Q7 G2 Q11 Q1

These eighteen stages correspond to the eighteen sections of Level I listed earlier:

1	2	3	5	6	7	9	10	11	13	14	15	17	18	19	21	22	23
D	Q12	Q4	E	Q8	Q2	E2	Q7	Q4	D2	Q3	Q11	L2	Q7	Q2	L	Q8	Q11
D	Q3	Q7	L	Q11	Q6	L2	Q5	Q7	D2	Q9	Q1	G	Q5	Q7	G2	Q11	Q1

One immediately notices that the one-to-one superimposition of these two particular paths suggests a division of the series into halves. This is the case since there are only two positions at which both paths reach the very same group elements - the first and tenth positions.

Next, it should be recalled that each of the twenty-four different elements in the octahedral group are represented as some permutation of eight numbers. Upon considering these permutations, one notices several important facts. First, all the permutations associated with the first twelve elements, I through L2, hold numbers 1, 2, 3 and 4 in the first four positions and 5, 6, 7 and 8 in the second four. Each group of four numbers are scrambled among themselves throughout the twelve permutations, but none of the first four ever mixes with any of the last four. Conversely, in all the permutations associated with the last twelve elements, Q1 through Q12, the numbers 1, 2, 3 and 4 are held in the last four positions and 5, 6, 7 and 8 are held in the first four. In other words, for

$$I \text{ through } L2 \quad : \quad (1,2,3,4) \quad (5,6,7,8)$$
$$Q1 \text{ through } Q12 \quad : \quad (5,6,7,8) \quad (1,2,3,4)$$

It is revealing to translate the two paths chosen above into the notation employed in constructing Chart B :

$$U1 = I,A...L2 \qquad U2 = Q1,Q2...Q12$$

$$V2oV4 = U1U2U2U1U2U2U1U2U2U1U2U2U1U2U2U1U2U2$$

$$V2oV5 = U1U2U2U1U2U2U1U2U2U1U2U2U1U2U2U1U2U2$$

Clearly, every third element belongs to U1 and all others to U2. As a result, both paths proceed in the following manner:

13

U1 (1,2,3,4) ✗ (5,6,7,8)
U2 (5,6,7,8) ⟩⟨ (1,2,3,4)
U2 (5,6,7,8) ⟋↘ (1,2,3,4)

U1 (1,2,3,4) ✗ (5,6,7,8)
U2 (5,6,7,8) ⟩⟨ (1,2,3,4)
U2 (5,6,7,8) ⟋↘ (1,2,3,4)

This procedure suggests a partitioning into sixths:

U1U2U2 U1U2U2 U1U2U2 U1U2U2 U1U2U2 U1U2U2

Next, it may be noted that within subgroup 1, letters I, A, B and C are their own inverses. In contrast, the inverses of D, E, G and L are, respectively, D2, E2, G2 and L2. Thus, each of the two chosen paths may be articulated by inverses in the following way:

DQQ EQQ E2QQ D2QQ L2QQ L QQ

DQQ LQQ L2QQ D2QQ GQQ G2QQ

This fact divides the path into two halves. Each half consists of three sets of group elements with three elements in each set:

123 123 123   123 123 123

1   2   3   1   2   3

Concerning the specific sonic materials by which these paths are articulated, V2 o V4 controls the transformation of sound gestures, and V2 o V5 controls the transformation of various internal characteristics of those gestures. In particular, with respect to Path V2 o V4, four different gestures are used:

a = an ordered collection of sounds, neither ascending nor descending

b = an ordered collection of sounds, ascending or descending

c = sustained sounds with aberrations

d = disordered collection of sounds, ascending or descending.

Each of these gestures is expressed in two different ways -

14

legato and staccato. Legato statements are generally played arco or arco tremolo (a1, b1, c1, d1), while staccato statements are played pizzicato or col legno battuto (a2, b2, c2, d2). These eight gestures are associated with the eight numbers of the permutations in three different ways:

	1	2	3	4	5	6	7	8
X	b2	a2	c2	d2	b1	a1	c1	d1
Y	c1	a1	b1	c2	a2	d1	d2	b2
Z	d2	c2	a2	a1	d1	c1	b2	b1

Clearly, in X the four staccato textures are associated with the numbers 1, 2, 3 and 4; and, the four legato textures with the numbers 5, 6, 7 and 8. As such, they will never mix. As a result of this mapping, the partitioning of the paths into groups of three will be clearly articulated.

A		Q		Q	
(1,2,3,4)	(5,6,7,8)	(5,6,7,8)	(1,2,3,4)	(5,6,7,8)...	
staccato	legato	legato	staccato	legato	...

The charts on the following three pages illustrate this point in more detail using the first three sections of the piece as examples.

Similarly, mappings Y and Z are so arranged as to give each half of the series three of one type of gesture and one of the other. As a result, even in Y and Z, one type of texture, either legato or staccato, still clearly predominates within each half. In Y, the first four are associated with three legato gestures, while the last four are associated with three staccato. In contrast, in Z, the first four are associated with three staccato gestures, while the last four are associated with three legato. Thus, each of the three mappings helps to articulate the division of eight numbers into two sets of four.

15

Section 1 (mm. 1 - 15):

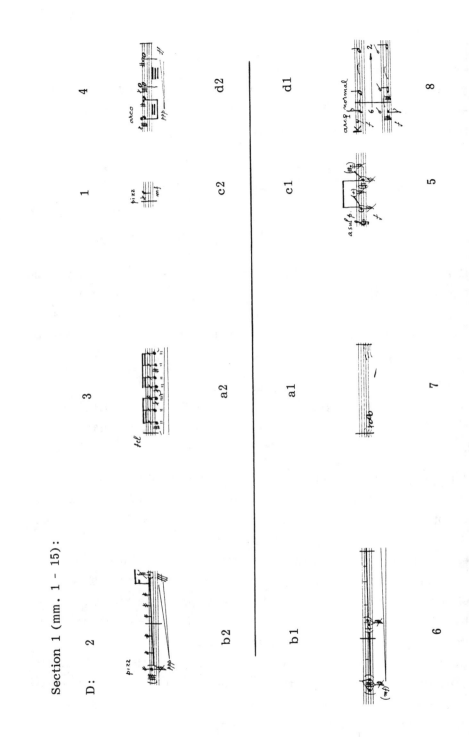

D: 2   3   1   4

      b2   a2   c2   d2

      ─────────────────

      b1   a1   c1   d1

6   7   5   8

Section 2 (mm. 16 - 30) :

Q12: 5

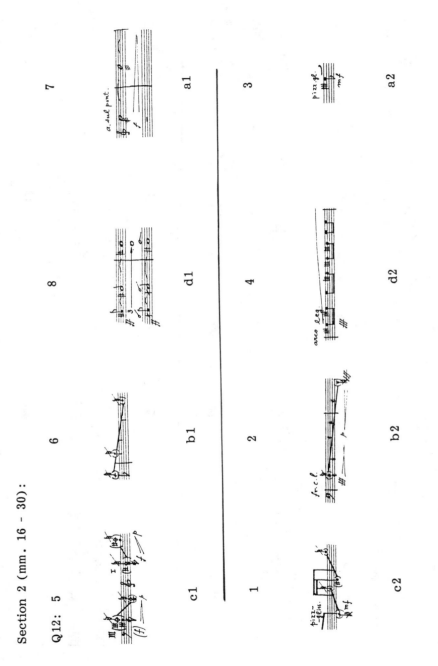

Section 3 (mm. 31 - 45):

Q4:

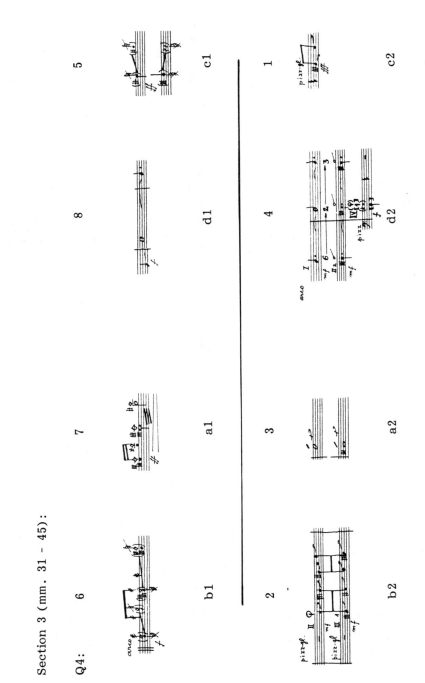

Finally, X, Y and Z are associated with Path V2 o V4 in the following way:

X	Y	Z	X	Y	Z
DQ12Q4	EQ8Q2	E2Q7Q4	D2Q3Q11	L2Q7Q2	LQ8Q11

Xenakis changes his mapping after every third section and then repeats his entire series of mappings after the ninth section, the mid-point, is reached. Clearly, this particular association further articulates the natural partition of the series into sixths and halves.

Path V2 o V5 is articulated sonically in the following way. Three parameters are defined and to each are assigned four values:

D (density)	G (volume)	U (duration)
d1	g1	u1
d2	g2	u2
d3	g3	u3
d4	g4	u4

From the triple product of these sets, eight points are chosen:

$$K1 = d1g1u1 \qquad K5 = d2g2u2$$
$$K2 = d1g4u4 \qquad K6 = d2g3u3$$
$$K3 = d4g4u4 \qquad K7 = d3g3u3$$
$$K4 = d4g1u1 \qquad K8 = d3g2u2$$

In each of these eight, g and u always have the same subscript. As such they may be re-written as:

$$K1 = d1(gu)1 \qquad K5 = d2(gu)2$$
$$K2 = d1(gu)4 \qquad K6 = d2(gu)3$$
$$K3 = d4(gu)4 \qquad K7 = d3(gu)3$$
$$K4 = d4(gu)1 \qquad K8 = d3(gu)2$$

From this chart it may be seen that the first four points, K1 through K4, are formed from all the possible combinations of the subscripts 1 and 4:

$$
\begin{array}{cc}
1 & 1 \\
1 & 4 \\
4 & 4 \\
4 & 1
\end{array}
$$

and the second four points are formed from all the possible combinations of 2 and 3:

$$
\begin{array}{cc}
2 & 2 \\
2 & 3 \\
3 & 3 \\
3 & 2
\end{array}
$$

Thus, by choosing these particular eight points, the composer ensures that the bipartite structure of the permutations, (1234) (5678), will also be articulated sonically in path V2 o V5.

In the set D (density), three different sets of values are employed:

	q	r	s
d1	.5	1	1
d2	1.08	2	1.5
d3	2.32	3	2
d4	5	4	2.5

The four elements in s are formed by steady increments of .5 and those of r by steady increments of 1. The four elements of q are formed exponentially. Thus, we actually have three sets of Ki's for Path V2 o V5:

$$
\begin{aligned}
&K\,1q = d1g1u1 && K\,2q = d1g4u4 && \cdots \\
&K\,1r = d1g1u1 && K\,2r = d1g4u4 && \cdots \\
&K\,1s = d1g1u1 && K\,2s = d1g4u4 && \cdots
\end{aligned}
$$

The values for G (intensity) and U (durations) are:

G	U
g1 - mf	u1 - 2"
g2 - f	u2 - 3"
g3 - ff	u3 - 4"
g4 - fff	u4 - 5"

The eight points Ki are associated with the eight numbers of each permutation. Finally, the three mappings q, r and s are associated with Path V2 o V5 in the following way:

q   r   s   q   r   s
DQ3Q7   LQ11Q6   L2Q5Q7   D2Q9Q1   GQ5Q7   G2Q11Q1

Once again, the particular association employed articulates the natural partition of the series into sixths and halves.

The chart on the following page summarizes the analysis presented thus far. Here all sets are unordered. Also, numerical values represent total density per event; that is, density per second multiplied by the total number of seconds.

Finally, the durations of the eighteen sections of level I reveal the following scheme:

Sections: 1 2 3 5 6 7 9 10 11 13 14 15 17 18 19 21 22 23

Durations
in
seconds: 24 24 24 21 18 22 32 33 31 24 25 26 23 23 24 31 35 27

Average
for every
group of
three
sections: 24   20   32   25   23   31

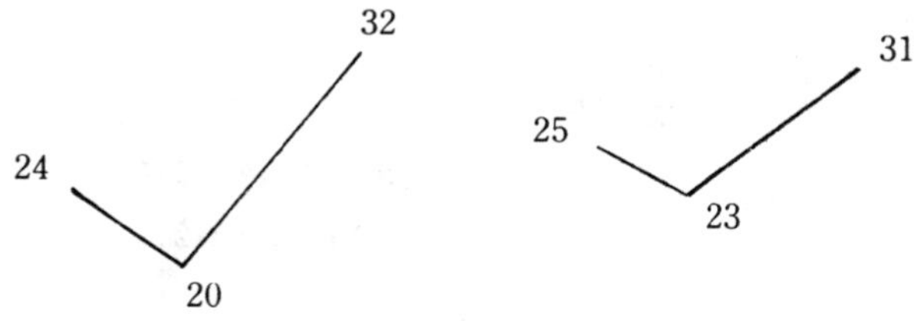

This scheme also suggests a division of the entire piece into halves, each of which is characterized by a temporal expansion.

Level II

The remaining six sections of the piece, which constitute

Sections

1	V2 o V4	(b1 b2 b3 b4)	(a1 a2 a3 a4)
2		(a1 a2 a3 a4)	(b1 b2 b3 b4)
3		(a1 a2 a3 a4)	(b1 b2 b3 b4)

1   V2 o V5
$$\begin{bmatrix} mf & fff \\ 2.2 & 22.5 & 1 & 10 \end{bmatrix} \times \begin{bmatrix} f & ff \\ 3.7 & 8 & 2.8 & 6 \end{bmatrix}$$

2
$$\begin{bmatrix} f & ff \\ 3.7 & 8 & 2.8 & 6 \end{bmatrix} \begin{bmatrix} mf & fff \\ 2.2 & 22.5 & 1 & 10 \end{bmatrix}$$

3
$$\begin{bmatrix} f & ff \\ 3.7 & 8 & 2.8 & 6 \end{bmatrix} \begin{bmatrix} mf & fff \\ 2.2 & 22.5 & 1 & 10 \end{bmatrix}$$

5	V2 o V4	(a1 a2 a3 b3)	(b1 b2 b4 a4)
6		(b1 b2 b4 a4)	(a1 a2 a3 b3)
7		(b1 b2 b4 a4)	(a1 a2 a3 b3)

5   V2 o V5
$$\begin{bmatrix} mf & fff \\ 2 & 14 & 8 & 4.5 \end{bmatrix} \times \begin{bmatrix} f & ff \\ 5.2 & 10.3 & 7.9 & 6.9 \end{bmatrix}$$

6
$$\begin{bmatrix} f & ff \\ 5.2 & 10.3 & 7.9 & 6.9 \end{bmatrix} \begin{bmatrix} mf & fff \\ 2 & 14 & 8 & 4.5 \end{bmatrix}$$

7
$$\begin{bmatrix} f & ff \\ 5.2 & 10.3 & 7.9 & 6.9 \end{bmatrix} \begin{bmatrix} mf & fff \\ 2 & 14 & 8 & 4.5 \end{bmatrix}$$

9	V2 o V4	(b1 b3 b4 a1)	(a2 a3 a4 b4)
10		(a2 a3 a4 b2)	(b1 b3 b4 a1)
11		(a2 a3 a4 b2)	(b1 b3 b4 a1)

9   V2 o V5
$$\begin{bmatrix} mf & fff \\ 2.5 & 4.5 & 11.3 \end{bmatrix} \times \begin{bmatrix} f & ff \\ 4 & 5.2 & 5.1 & 6.9 \end{bmatrix}$$

10
$$\begin{bmatrix} f & ff \\ 3.9 & 5.2 & 5.1 & 6.9 \end{bmatrix} \begin{bmatrix} mf & fff \\ 2.5 & 4.5 & 11.3 \end{bmatrix}$$

11
$$\begin{bmatrix} f & ff \\ 3.9 & 5.2 & 5.1 & 6.9 \end{bmatrix} \begin{bmatrix} mf & fff \\ 2.5 & 4.5 & 11.3 \end{bmatrix}$$

etc.

22

level II, are striking in their apparent dissimilarity to those of level I. These sections - 4, 8, 12, 16, 20 and 24 - are not based on a group structure. Rather, they constitute one continuous evolution of register.

First, it should be noted that these six sections differ in both dynamics and register from those of level I. In particular, level I falls within the mid-range of the cello and employs closely related dynamic levels - mf, f, ff and fff. Level II, in contrast, focuses on the extremities of the instrument's range and striking dynamic contrasts - pppp, pp, ff and fff.

In terms of duration, the six sections of the second level reveal the following scheme:

Sections: 4   8   12   16   20   24

Durations in seconds: 30   22   15   22   30   35

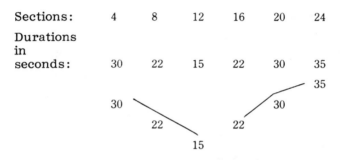

which, once again, suggests a division into two halves.

As stated earlier, however, the primary evolution which constitutes the structure of these six sections concerns register. The gestures employed are very simple: long sustained tones and glissandi. The former are used to establish plateaus in various registers; the latter, to shift from one of these plateaus to another. Within each section, all gestures are completely fused to form one or more broad sweeping motions. For example, in section 8, there are two such continuous motions, each in contrary motion to the other. This section in particular prepares the two expansive gestures, also in contrary motion, found at the very end of the piece.

The overall spatial movement of level II is outlined in the

23

following chart:[3]

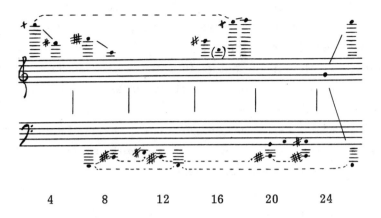

4	8	12	16	20	24

Sections 4, 8 and 12 project one large descent from D^+8 to $C1$ with one, contrary ascending motion in section 8. Significantly, this brief motion begins on $C1$, thereby anticipating the goal of the descent within which it is subsumed. In the second half, sections 16 and 20 focus, respectively, on the cello's high and low registers. While, in the first half, these extremes are connected through one continuous movement, in the second half all connections are severed. Each is presented as a separate plateau, isolated from the other. Significantly, section 16 employs no glissandi and section 20, only one. Glissandi are the means through which different registers are connected and no such connection is desired here. The final section of the second half, and of the entire piece, section 24, once again unites the highest and lowest registers, and recaptures the more continuous motion which characterized sections 4, 8 and 12. Section 24 begins on a unison $G4$ in the middle of the cello's range and proceeds to travel three octaves and a fifth in both directions, simultaneously recapturing both the highest and lowest points of the piece (the D^+8 reached at the beginning of section 4 and the $C1$ reached at the end of section 8). Thus, the final section summarizes the entire spatial motion of the piece on level II and once again unites the two plateaus isolated in sections 16 and 20. This is summarized in the following chart:

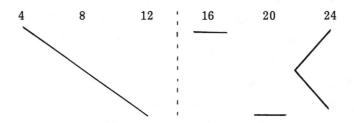

| 4 | 8 | 12 | 16 | 20 | 24 |

Before concluding, some comments on the pitch structure of the composition would be appropriate. However, any detailed discussion of pitch would involve an explication of a branch of mathematics known as sieve theory which unfortunately, space does not permit. For the purposes of this paper, suffice it to say that a series of twelve interrelated pitch collections are used in the piece. These are presented in accordance with the following format:

levels I and II

1 2 3	5 6 7	9 10 11	13 14 15	17 18 19	21 22 23
4	8	12	16	20	24
1	2 3	4 5	6 7	8 9	10 11	12

pitch collections

From just this much information, it may be observed that the assignment of pitch collections to sections serves to further articulate the partitioning of the sequence of eighteen sections on level I into groups of three; and helps to separate the two levels. The former is accomplished through the use of a single pitch collection for every three sections of the first level. The latter is accomplished through the introduction of a new collection at those moments when the composition shifts from one level to the other.

Observations

In comparing his work to that of a younger colleague,

25

Milton Babbitt, Edgard Varese once observed:

> It seems to me that he wants to exercise maximum control over certain materials as if he were above them. But I want to be in the material, part of the acoustical vibration...[4]

Within the framework of this single composition, Xenakis identifies the same differences of morphology as those rather poetically formulated by Varese. In *Nomos Alpha*, he explores the relationship of a structure to the materials which engender that structure. One part of the composition presents a structure borrowed from mathematics and determined apart from any interaction with the sonic materials employed. The other, in contrast, is a direct and organic outgrowth of the composer's manipulation of those materials.

With respect to level I, a structure is created prior to and independent of the choice of the specific sounds employed. More precisely, as may be clear from the analysis presented above, the materials are chosen and shaped only that they may clearly articulate various aspects of the mathematical group from which the sonic structure is derived. Specifically, one permutation group is applied to a variety of materials. The two paths employed are not only structurally identical but, in fact, share many elements. They control, independently, on the one hand, the parameters of dynamics, duration and density; and, on the other hand, the nature and timbre of each gesture.

In many works, the processes of transformation which guide the music's evolution are in some way engendered by the specific materials employed. As such, their unfolding is tied, in specific ways, to the qualities and characteristics of those materials. On level I, in contrast, these processes (the permutation schemes) are broad and inclusive and, as such, capable of operating on a wide range of dissimilar materials.[5] Thus, the structure of level I is characterized by certain qualities of abstraction which are

26

quite in keeping with the abstract nature of the mathematical structures themselves. On level II, however, one finds a striking contrast to this compositional approach. The structure of this part of the work is as rooted in its sonic materials as that of level I is independent of them. Here, form emerges from the direct manipulation of materials by the composer. Indeed, on level II, form is identified with those very processes by which the materials are shaped and transformed. The structure of this level, therefore, involves not so much the shaping of materials to fit some pre-determined mold, but rather, the unfolding of a continuous evolutionary process in which the nature of the materials themselves plays a crucial, formative role.

It is interesting to note that level I is an example of a discrete structure while level II is, essentially, a continuous one. On level I, eight distinct elements are defined for each parameter and then used to articulate the permutation schemes. In contrast, on level II, all sonic elements are tied to one another within an unbroken temporal/spatial continuum. In fact, with respect to the structure of level II, it would seem more correct to speak of a single continuously evolving shape than a collection of discrete elements united in some atomistic manner. Indeed, the two rather disparate notions of discrete and continuous seem apt metaphors with which to consider the essential dialectical thrust of the piece.

The form of *Nomos Alpha*, then, would appear to have as its source the juxtaposition of two radically different methodologies. From their interaction a magnificent dialogue evolves, over the course of which some of the most important issues concerning the evolution of structure are addressed and illuminated.

Appendix

For those familiar with group theory, it may be interesting to recall that the twenty-four permutations employed in *Nomos Alpha* can be derived from the twenty-four isometries of the cube. The folowing chart, borrowed from the composer's own analysis, depicts all twenty-four possible rotations of a cube:

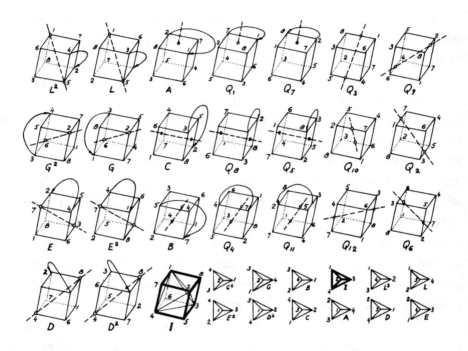

It is fascinating, in light of the preceding analysis, to recall certain relationships between the cube and the tetrahedron. The natural partitioning of each permutation into two groups of four elements has its roots in the fact that the tetrahedron may be inscribed within the cube in only two different ways:

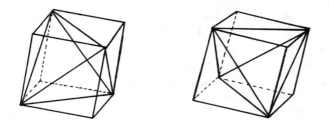

This, of course, suggests that, as the cube is rotated in space, certain adjacencies are preserved. If the cube is rotated in any of the following twelve ways: I, A, B, C, D, D2, E, E2, G, G2, L and L2, all the points labeled 1, 2, 3 and 4 will exchange positions only among themselves. In contrast, if the cube is rotated in any of the remaining twelve ways: Q1, Q2, Q3, Q4, Q5, Q6, Q7, Q8, Q9, Q10, Q11 and Q12, all the points labeled 1, 2, 3 and 4 will exchange positions with those labeled 5, 6, 7 and 8 and, of course, vice-versa. Thus, some of the most important properties of the twenty-four permutations explored by the composer in level I of the composition are derived from basic geometric properties of the cube.

1) Iannis Xenakis, *Formalized Music* (Bloomington, Indiana: Indiana University Press, 1971), pp. 219 - 236.

2) Those readers with some background in mathematics will immediately recognize that subgroups 1 and 2 are both normal; that sets U_i ($i=1,2$) and V_j ($j=1,2...6$) are the cosets of these subgroups; and, that Charts B and C are, respectively, the quotient groups for subgroups 1 and 2.

3) All tones below C3 shown on this chart are produced by tuning (scordatura) the C string of the cello down one octave.

4) Edgard Varese, "Conversation with Varese" (Edgard Varese in conversation with Gunther Schuller) *Perspectives on American Composers*, Benjamin Boretz and Edward Cone, eds. (New York: W. W. Norton, 1971), p. 38

5) Indeed, this same structure of permutations has been used by the composer in a very different piece, *Nomos Gamma* for large orchestra (see *Formalized Music*, pp. 236 - 241). In this work, the same group is applied to an even broader range of materials and textures.

"Charm'd Magic Casements"

Pozzi Escot

How does it happen that we create? Jacob Bronowski writes that "discoveries of science (and) works of art are explorations... explosions of a hidden likeness."[1] All around us there is but a hint of what nature hides; the philosopher of science and mathematics Hermann Weyl, refers to the loveliness hidden under the surface beauty of nature - that the mathematics is not to be revealed in its skin. Biologist Gregory Bateson recognizes that our minds are but mirrors of nature.[2] Yet, how does it happen that we begin to explore? There must be an ability to find that likeness, to recognize it, to grasp it, to pry it, and, eventually, to reproduce and convey it with challenging means and explosive invention.

From where comes the ability? From where comes the resource to convey the discovery? As tools are acquired, mastery, control, and refinement are learned. But, the substantial imagination and unique vision - the drive and discipline - are not. Assuming that an intelligent mind is available, not even favorable circumstances of life are a requisite. It suffices to have the ability.

Still, how do we create? From where come the chants of von Bingen, the designs of Kandinsky, the sonic constructions of Ligeti? What is the likeness that we create? English mathematician H. E. Huntly says that it is a type of beauty which must have certain ingredients:[3]

31

alternation of tension and relief

realization of expectation

perception of unsuspected relationships

brevity ('redundancyless')

unity

joy

sense of wonder

This beauty is that hidden likeness which an artist sees in an abundant experience. In *The Education of the Whole Man*, Lawrence Pearsall Jacks asks:

What then is the vocation of...man?

...to be a creator

...of what?

...of real values.

...what motives can be appealed to,

...what driving power can be relied on, to bring out the creative element in men and women?

...love of beauty, innate in everybody..."[4]

Aristotle also mentions this hidden likeness. He says that art imitates, then arranges imitation in temporally and spatially patterned structures, completing or giving finishing touches to what nature has left incomplete. It is creativity as re-casting. The Greeks pointed out five principles of art:

1) art-catharsis: creativity must re-create in unfathomable ways

2) art-significance: creativity must have overriding information

3) art-arrangement: creativity must have overwhelming structure

4) art-quality: creativity must be above the ordinary

5) art-involvement: creativity must bring

forth challenging participation.

The ability is a relationship between unconscious and controlled intelligence. An amorphous flashed-image expands toward molded expression and effective art. It is the wise teacher Aspasia who tells Socrates that what is beautiful is difficult. The ability is an energy.

Every bit of art has its own reality. This is a reality which obeys a skill; a skill permeated with timing. This is a reality that must be recovered. And what can that reality be? If art is exploration and explosion of a hidden likeness that the perceiver has created, then there is the reader and listener who must attempt to unravel that re-hidden likeness. Who must find the proportions and study the dimensions to discover the construction? For the hidden likeness, imitation is discreet.

In music, the hidden likeness is not an immediate result. The relationships of essential components in the composition of music can indeed be complex and magical. A myriad of aspects are combined to conquer an architectural sonic design, the hidden proportions of which often reveal stupendous spatial deployments. In a letter dated 1934, answering a request by a Mr. Koons from NBC for a definition of what music is, Arnold Schoenberg wrote:

> Music is a simultaneous and a successive-ness of tones and tone combinations, which are so organized that its impression on the ear is agreeable, and its impression on the intelligence is comprehensible, and that these impressions have the power to influence occult parts of our soul and of our sentimental spheres...I know a nice and touching story:
> A blind man asked his guide: 'How looks milk?'
> The guide answered: 'Milk looks white.'

33

The blind man: 'What's that 'white'?
Mention a thing which is white!'
The guide: 'A swan. It is perfect white,
and it has a long white and bent neck.'
The blind man: '...a bent neck? How is
that?'
The guide, imitating with his arm the form
of a swan's neck, lets the blind man feel
the form of his arm.
The blind man (flowing softly with his
hand along the arm of the guide): 'Now I
know how looks milk.'[5]

Ligeti Looks Back - Hildegard von Bingen's Antiphon No. 38, "De Virginibus"

The antiphon "De Virginibus" (ca. 1140), is an example of duly proportioned dimensions.[6] The antiphon has three sections and thirteen phrases. The ranges of these thirteen phrases draw an almost retrogradable pyramid which can be seen as radial symmetry when the seventh phrase is isolated at its core.

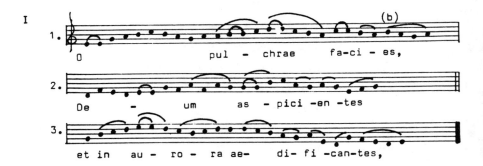

II

4. O be - a - tae vir-gi -nes,

5. quam nobi - les e - stis.

6. In qui - bus Rex

7. se con - sidera- vit,

8. cum in vo - bis

9. o - mni - a caele -sti -a or - na -men - ta

10. prae - si -gnavit,

III

11. u- bi et- i-am suavissimus hortus estis,

12. in o- mni- bus or- namen- tis

red- olen-

13. tes.

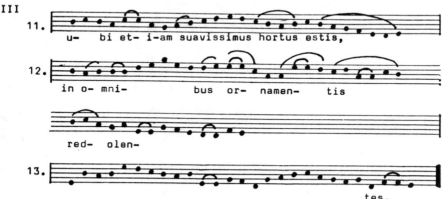

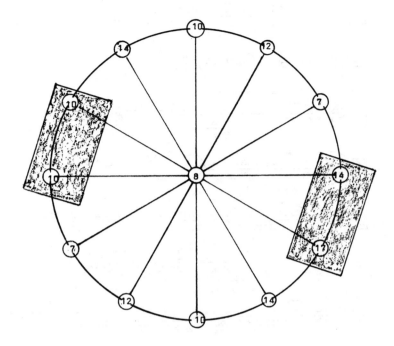

Phrase seven, with the unique range of an 8 (B4-G5), sounds a differentiated characterization:

    a) a tetratonic note collection

    b) the highest pitch of the antiphon for the first time; isolating the high G5 by approaching it with a 5 and leaving it with a 3

    c) the most dense ratio of syllables per pitch (one, two or three pitches per syllable)

    d) highest register

    e) the most E's, a pitch which dominates the beginnings and endings of phrases, and anticipates its priority in the second half of the chant.

This phrase, which is followed by the shortest phrase, divides the antiphon into two parts with a similar ratio of attacks per syllable, 2.8. One other bipartite division occurs at the negative Golden Section, the completion of phrase five, where the text ends its laudable address to the virgin. Thus, the antiphon presents, simultaneously, a dual bipartite and sectional tripartite division:

I   II

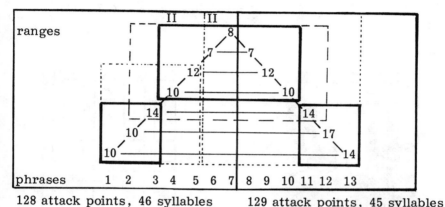

phrases   1 2   3 4   5 6 7   8 9 10 11 12 13
128 attack points, 46 syllables   129 attack points, 45 syllables

□ = bipartite division (syllable ratio) , ⊡ = bipartite division (negative Golden Section) , ◼ = tripartite division, ⌐⌐ = exact retrogradable pyramid

1) O pulcrae facies,

2) Deum aspicientes

3) et in aurora aedificantes,

4) O beatae virgines,

5) quam nobiles estis.

6) In quibus Rex

7) se consideravit,

8) cum in vobis

9) omnia caelestia ornamenta

10) praesignavit,

11) ubi etiam suavissimus hortus estis,

12) in omnibus ornamentis redolen-

13) -tes

A graphing of the ranges reveals an architectural facade which depicts both the bipartite and tripartite quasi-symmetrical divisions; wherein the seemingly non-proportional far sides (beginning phrases of ranges 10 and 10, and ending phrases of 17 and 14) are the additive numbers of the exact symmetrical body:

$$14 + 10 + 12 + 7 + 8 = 51$$
$$51 = 20 \, (10 + 10) + 31 \, (17 + 14)$$

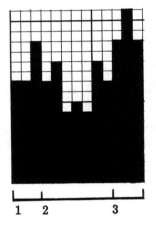

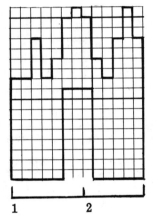

Moreover, the sums of these two pairs (20 and 31) have a mean of .618; thus, 20 and 31 partition 51 according to the Golden Section.

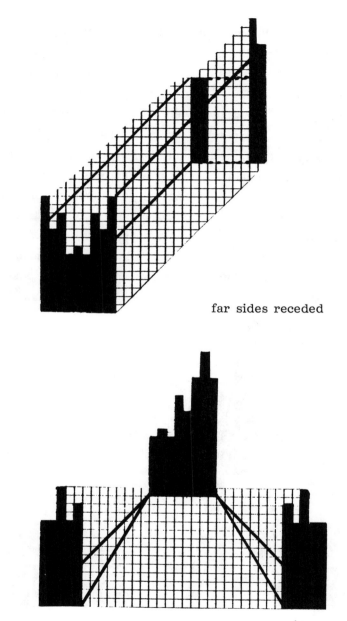

far sides receded

negative Golden Section   mirror

The proportions found among the number of attacks per frequency reveal another hidden likeness of dynamic symmetry. The seven frequencies of the linguistic collection which is heard are arranged in equidistant priorities of a 7 with a 6 between the most and least sounding priority - a non-tempered circle of fifths extraordinary for the period (twelfth century); albeit, extraordinary for Ligeti over eight hundred years later (see below). The exception in the priority stress is the pitch E which has six less attacks than its successor A. However, E is a final and, of all the frequencies, it is present at starting and ending points the most out of the twenty-six available possibilities. At twelve times, only the pitch B comes close, eight times taking over beginnings and endings of phrases. Furthermore, E is the most sustained frequency, sounding nine times (compared with only three for A). Thus, in terms of priority position, E supersedes the pitch A.

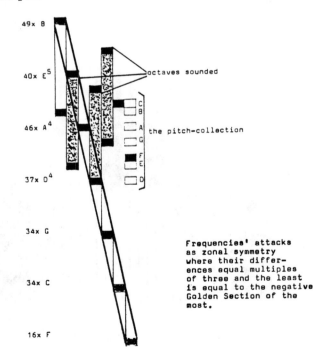

49x B

40x E⁵

octaves sounded

46x A⁴

the pitch-collection

37x D⁴

34x G

34x C

16x F

Frequencies' attacks
as zonal symmetry
where their differ-
ences equal multiples
of three and the least
is equal to the negative
Golden Section of the
most.

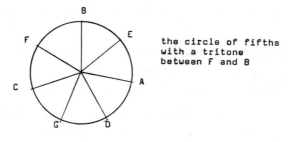

the circle of fifths
with a tritone
between F and B

The Golden Section dynamic symmetry can be traced in the inner-interplay of the antiphon's phrases. In the first section, for example, the following proportions are present:

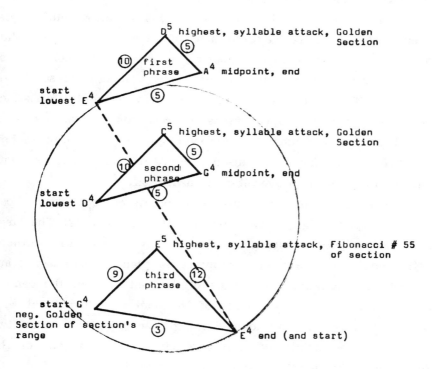

In painting, a secret geometry is an essential component. The hidden internal construction is not necessarily evident to the eye's first or second impressions; nor are the formulas which control those forms eventually evident to the mind. Again, it is analysis and study that begins to disclose the work's schema. As we look at *Dessin* No.21 (1932) of Kandinsky, four events appear to disengage the framework. Two events seem static while the other two present amorphous movement. Of the two static events, one satisfies and strives to outline a precise structure. It is a self-centered shape with little relation to the rather curved and incomplete forms of the other three, for its linear contours engage in their own interplay. The central and largest event is a vertical aggregation of five slices - a solid, dimensional, curved item appearing to possess no concern for lateral and north-south happenings. And, although the south one shows itself curtailing or directing the central event's formation, both the other two appear recessed from this central figure. A deciphering of the hidden geometry begins to shed light on how these four non-linear, or disconnected, drawings can associate and become part of an overall commensuration.

Using very specific positions as points of departure we can trace two plane figures encompassing the four events. The large isosceles triangle encloses the central event and its southern reflection. The five points mapping its plane measurements are the upper, sideways boundaries of the last slice of the central event, and the two end points of the double arched event with its focal tangent. The long rectangle encloses the other two events. Three points of each determine the dimensions of the rectangle. The middle, inner vertex of the first slice fixes the ninety-degree angle of the radii of the circumference, which flanks the top of the triangle and the right upper edge of the rectangle; thus confirming their respective proportions. The

Dessin No. 21 (1932)
Wassily Kandinsky

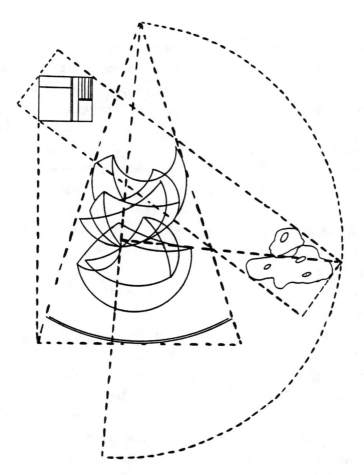

diameter intersects the lower, larger side of the rectangle and the base of the triangle at their respective Golden Sections. The radius is equal to the Golden Section of the larger sides of the rectangle. Still another balance between the two traced, plane, geometrical figures is the radius-sized line joining the left, lower angle of the Mondrian-styled figure and the left angle at the base of the triangle.

From this closed-up, unseen geometry, the unfavorable disconnection noted earlier begins to dissolve into a discipline of interrelationships - the lines and curves of the four events thereby acquiring a contextual kinship. A glimpsed perspective arises; not of foreground and background, not of dimensional illumination, but of ambiguity. It is a multi-dimensional perspective absolving a variety of seemingly independent events: some solid, some plane, some curved and infinite, some linear and finite, some set in motion, some static, some amorphous, some formal; all interacting in perfectly measured places to project a multi-faceted composition.

Symmetry and geometry played an important role in Greek thought. The Pythagoreans concluded that proportional number patterns determined the essence of all things. According to Plato, "The mathematical laws governing nature are the origin of symmetry in nature; the intuitive realization of the idea (of symmetry) in the creative mind; (and) its origin in art (and scientific research)."[7] The small and large scale correlation of parts to its whole appear then to be the imperative drive to mirror the hidden likeness already dispersed around us. Jacob Bronowski writes that Leonardo Da Vinci was occupied with the logic of the processes he saw in people and machines; and he looked for their hidden structure because it expressed logic, proportion and symmetry.

Now it is time to discuss Ligeti and his development of dynamic symmetry.

The composer Gyorgy Ligeti arrived in the western part of Europe from Hungary after the upheavals in that country in 1956. It was around this period - the composer then in his late twenties - that he first conceived the idea of a static, self-contained music; a music propelled to growth via dynamic symmetries in almost miraged ways. How this initial conception of creating sonic intelligence finally crystallizes in his works of the sixties is indeed an experience to hear, see and analyze.

With the vision of an architect, Ligeti dominates his musical expression - the measured parts become somewhat unreal and enter the world of "charm'd magic casements" (Keats quoted by Ligeti)[8] as the seemingly erratic sonic mosaics that make up the composition of his sonic canvases continually oscillate in order to merge, disperse and die out. The sounds of these casements exist through the aggregation of strands where insinuating canonic motion threads a web of phantom-like strata, the contours of which are generated by specific frequencies set in motion by the perfectly gauged parts.

Works like *Continuum*, *Lux Aeterna* and *Harmonies* are monuments imagined and qualified by a complex geometry; allowing only the surveyor to reconstitute their hidden proportions back toward logical manifestation after thorough scrutiny. A multitude of configurations is designed to sustain the harmony of these monuments, flowing through in correct sizes, shaping the buildings anew for each performance. The collaboration of the mosaics converges toward a unity of constant adaptation to the overall rules of the initial invention. Yet the architecture does not subordinate the search of Ligeti for color transformation. The *al fresco* impression soon gives room to contrasts deriving from the lines governing the total architecture of the work. It is the hidden geometry, which supports the nuances and the numbers outlining this geometric timing, that produces a subtle array of colors.

It was in the work for organ, *Harmonies* (1967), that Ligeti at last amalgamated static sound with an equally static architecture. In this work, ten simultaneous strands - all with canonic parity - inch their way, one attack at a time, never sounding two attacks from different strands together; and drawing a slight and slow widening of an original 23 to a 33, after which a more marked narrowing motion begins to a final 3. Again the motion is symmetrical, moving upwards and downwards: a 5 to the 33; and, a 15 to the 3. This bi-lateralism is numerically related through the value five: 33 - 28 - 23 - 18 - 13 - (8) - 3; and 15 - 10 - 5.

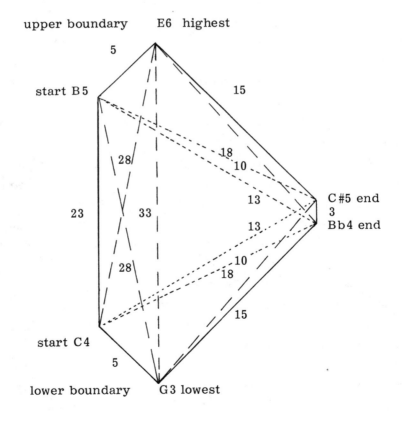

46

The ten voices of *Harmonies* span two hundred and thirty-one units of one attack each. The voices move with parallel finger-exchange in exact cumulative addition from one to two hundred and thirty-one:

PHRASES:

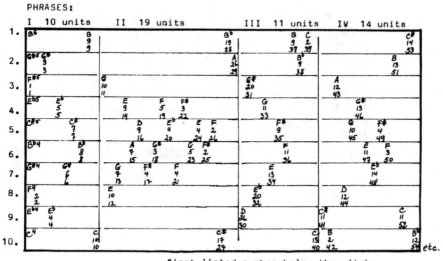

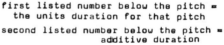

first listed number below the pitch =
the units duration for that pitch

second listed number below the pitch =
additive duration

47

To overview this display we can obtain, through a one-to-one reduction, the following space/time diagram which pictures the interactions between the parallel voices:

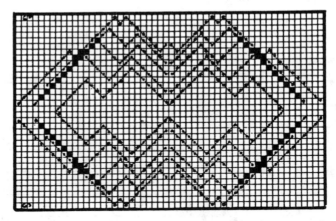

one horizontal square = each pitch in one-to-one reduction
one vertical square = one pitch of the chromatic collection

If we complete the outlined hidden geometry, of which Ligeti used only two thirds, the symmetry becomes even more obvious:

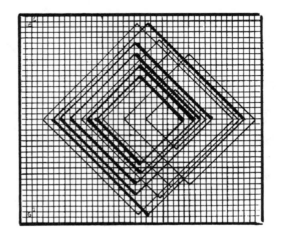

The following two charts convey fully the amazing statistics of symmetry found in the composition:

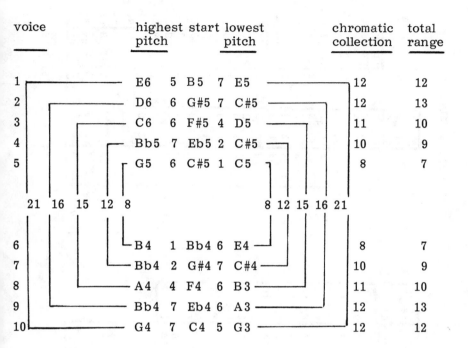

voice	highest pitch	start	lowest pitch			chromatic collection	total range
1	E6	5	B5	7	E5	12	12
2	D6	6	G#5	7	C#5	12	13
3	C6	6	F#5	4	D5	11	10
4	Bb5	7	Eb5	2	C#5	10	9
5	G5	6	C#5	1	C5	8	7
21 16 15 12 8				8 12 15 16 21			
6	B4	1	Bb4	6	E4	8	7
7	Bb4	2	G#4	7	C#4	10	9
8	A4	4	F4	6	B3	11	10
9	Bb4	7	Eb4	6	A3	12	13
10	G4	7	C4	5	G3	12	12

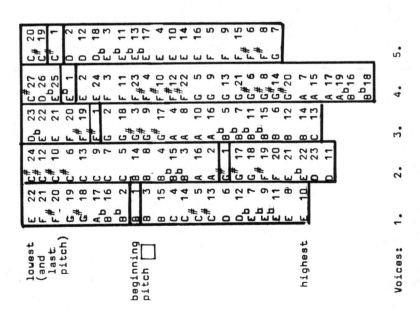

50

Recalling Hildegard von Bingen's antiphon, a similar quasi-retrogradable pyramid of phrases as well as a pitch priority sequence are found in Ligeti's composition. The phrases, while gently juxtaposed through continuous sonic design, are recognized through the canonic parity and motion of the ten voices with occasional slight interchanging of the pairs (which, in the following diagram, are not underlined):

```
Phrases                Voice Attacks                          Units

 1      0  3-8  2-9  4-7  5-6  1-                               10
 2        10  3-8  7-4  6-5  7-6 -4-5  7-4  6-5  6-5  10-1      19
 3      2-9  3-8  4-7  5-6  1-2 -1-                             11
 4      10-9-10  3-8  5-4 -6-7  5-6  2-9  1-                    14
 5        10  3-8  10-1  9-2  7-4  6-5  8-3  7-4  1-            16
 6        10  5-6  5-6  4-7  3-8  2-9  1-                       12
 7        10  4-3 -7-8 -2-1 -9-10                                9
 8      4-7  2-9  3-8  3-8  4-7  8-7 -3-9 -4-2  7-4  9-2
                   8-3  7-4  5-6  5-6  7-4  5-6  1-             33
 9        10  2-9  4-7  3-8  7-7 -8-4 -4-3  4-7  2-9  1-        18
10        10  3-8  5-6  2-9  7-10-6-4 -1-                       12
11      5  4-3 -2-7 -8-9  8-3  2-9  10-1  1-                    14
12      5 -4-10-6-7  8-3  1-3 -2-1-                             11
13      2-10-8-9-10-4 -9-7 -1-2-10-9  5-6  5-6  3-8  1-         19
14        10  4-7  2-9  3-8  1-10  2-9  4-7  3-8  1-            16
15        10  2-9  1-10  0-0  0-0  9-2  0-0  2-9  0-0           17
```

Thus, we obtain:

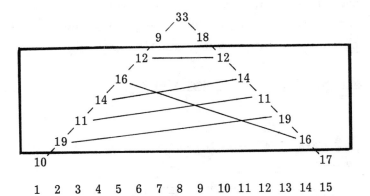

1 2 3 4 5 6 7 8 9 10 11 12 13 14 15

phrases

wherein the seemingly non-proportional beginning and ending phrases of ten and seventeen units, respectively, and the phrases before and after the apex of the pyramid (nine and eighteen units), are related as follows:

$$10 + 17 = 27$$
$$27 = 9 + 18$$

Their corresponding addition is the negative Golden Section of the balanced inner phrases' total (although permuted in their retrogression):

$$19 + 11 + 14 + 16 + 12 = 72$$
$$72 = 12 + 14 + 11 + 19 + 16$$
$$72 \times .382 = 27$$
$$27 = (10+17) \text{ or } (9+18)$$

and, the addition of these two pairs of phrases relates in a Golden Section ratio to the apex phrase of thirty-three units:

$$27 + 27 = 54$$
$$54 \times .618 = 33$$

The fifteen phrases, drawing an almost retrogradable pyramid, can be seen as radial symmetry when the apex phrase of thirty-three units is isolated as its core:

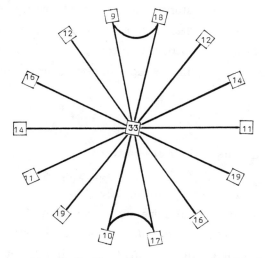

The proportion of the frequency of attacks is another hidden likeness of dynamic symmetry:

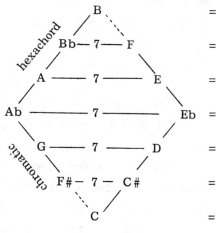

pitch attack:

= 17x (starting upper pitch)

= 19x

= 20x

= 21x

= 20x

= 19x

= 17x (starting lower pitch)

53

This colossal construction has no recesses, no moments of relaxation; only active balances of fluctuation. Its duration projects an exciting listening experience. Such formal symmetry, however, provides constant ambiguity stemming out of what appears to be mere rotation on a fixed axis. In its small scale formation of static and vibrant forces, an almost imperceptible opposition results - this effect creating the drama 'of the composition.

A pattern of patterns - the meta-pattern;

The biologist Gregory Bateson notes that being responsive to a pattern which connects means developing the critical aspect and the aesthetic experience. *Harmonies* is strata of connective patterns not just describing a nicety, but involving a remarkable invention and recalling the ability to fulfill it. As mentioned before, Pythagoreans regarded symmetric number patterns as the essence of all things. Ligeti's "charm'd magic casements" are the logic-processed numbers of a hidden structure. As in Hildegard von Bingen's antiphon, "De Virginibus," and Kandinsky's *Dessin* No. 21, time and space are traced by accurate measurements in a large scale canvas of single, moving, equally-sized dots. The one-to-one relationship found in the linguistic motion (the chromatic inching of its ten voices) stresses this step-by-step onward march. The rich spectra of the organ sound constantly mars this bare clarity, thus greatly reducing the sense of its meager motion and seldom lifting the listener ahead. The static denouement is a total compendium of forces - the audition almost failing to grasp the fortress behind. A chain of interrelated symmetries produces the effect of equal recurrence. The pattern of patterns becomes a nebulous constellation of sonic design.

The Graph of *Harmonies*

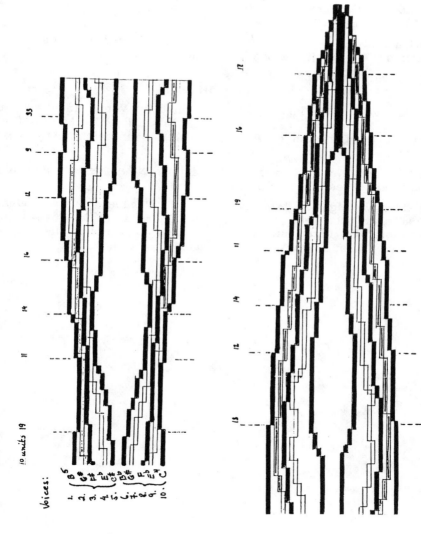

1) Jacob Bronowski, *Science and Human Values* (London: Pelican, 1964), p. 29.

2) Gregory Bateson, *Mind and Nature* (New York: Dutton, 1979).

3) H. E. Huntley, *The Divine Proportion* (New York: Dover, 1970), pp. 81 - 89.

4) Lawrence Pearsall Jacks, *The Education of the Whole Man* (London: University of London Press, 1952).

5) Arnold Schoenberg, *Letters*, edited by Erwin Stein (New York: St. Martin's Press, 1965), p. 186.

6) Hildegard von Bingen, *Chants*, edited by Von Prudentia Barth OSB, M. Immaculata Ritscher OSB and Joseph Schmidt-Gorg (Salzburg: Otto Muller Verlag, 1969), transcription by Pozzi Escot.

7) Hermann Weyl, *Symmetry* (Princeton, New Jersey: Princeton University Press, 1952), p. 8.

8) Gyorgy Ligeti, "About Lontano," *Donaueschingen Journal* (1967),pp. 68 - 91. The phrase, "Charm'd Magic Casements," as quoted by Ligeti in "About Lontano," is found in the English poet John Keat's "Ode To a Nightingale," written in 1819.

Penetrating Ensembles

Robert Cogan

I Introduction

Electronically synthesized music - a vortex of challenges and possibilities: a potential of riches which Milton Babbitt was one of the first and most eager to tap. This potential poses, in itself, a novel challenge to composers, music theorists, and listeners. The riches, with their unruly abundance of sounds and sound formations drawn from the entire humanly audible ranges of frequency and intensity (occasionally even bursting beyond them); with their abundance of any and all conceivable sonic durations, extending from the infinitesimal to the forseeably (or unforseeably) eternal; and with their abundance of the most diverse imaginable tone colors and attendant sound spectrum configurations - these abundant riches now pour beyond the limits of any and every prior attempt at musical self-definition and understanding as developed in previously existing theoretical systems. Even so resourceful a theorist as Babbitt himself has not, as far as I know, offered a substantial view of his own conceptual system of electronic sound or tone color. And if he had, we cannot expect that it would necessarily solve our problems of attaining sonic understanding, either of his *Ensembles for Synthesizer* or of any other electronic work. Indeed, were he to accomplish this, he might well be the first composer in all music history to entirely solve the conceptual challenges posed by his or her own music. This is an unlikely, probably even logically unattainable, solution.

We ourselves are left to meet the challenge, which is to envision a framework for understanding that encompasses and embraces the superabundant sonic possibilities of the electronic medium. And then, to place all of the details and relationships of any individual piece in terms of such an all-encompassing vision. Viewed in this way, the problem turns out not so very different from the other novel theoretical challenge of our time, that posed by global music as a whole, which also requires an all-encompassing framework and the precise placement of any specific music within it.[1]

A particular quality of the beginning of Babbitt's *Ensembles* is how, with a few exemplary sounds lasting in total less than one minute (fifty-six seconds, to be exact), a whole sonic universe is summoned up. The piece's beginning sketches, exactly and concisely, a sonic framework for all that follows. Consequently, we shall give it our full attention, not once, but rather twice: first in a less, and then again in a more, formal view. Even so, I would like immediately to stress that the two views do not aim at "completeness". Rather, we are directing our attention especially toward what has previously been, and still remains, most elusive in musical understanding: the qualities and relationships of musical sound *per se* - sonic relationships, sometimes construed as tone color relationships. While even in the past these relationships have almost always eluded understanding, here in electronic music we are further deprived of the single, albeit unsatisfactory, crutch previously available in tone color discussion, namely musical instruments and an instrumental conception of tone color.

During the past decade many colleagues and I, working together, have tried to describe and then to fill this gap in musical sonic awareness, a gap that exists not only for electronic music, but which has existed for virtually all musics and for

58

every individual piece of music. This essay depends on, and will hardly repeat, what has already appeared in those previous writings.[2] In them it has emerged (following clues provided by such scientific analysts of sound as Helmholtz and Mach) that sonic qualities depend upon the elements of the sound spectrum, and upon their deployment through part or all of the ten-register sonic space audible to all humans. Just recently the acoustical spatio-spectral analysis of musical sounds has been greatly furthered by the development of sound spectrum analysis facilities that reveal the spectral elements and their space-time deployment in music with extraordinary sensitivity, clarity, and speed.[3] We will use a photo of such an analysis of Babbitt's *Ensembles*, the sound spectrum photo shown in Figure 1, in order to discern its particular spectral elements as they sound in time and space.

To this spatio-spectral analysis has most recently been added a second level of awareness: that the sonic elements bear certain specific relations, functions, and values in any given context, as they create its specific sound shape. In a context, the set of features of any sonic moment, is either like the set of features of any other sonic moment, or it is (in part, or in totality) unlike and opposed to it. By analysis and subsequent comparison of the sets of features of successive sonic moments of a work, there emerges a view of the similarities and oppositions of those moments (those morphologies) to each other; and finally a view of the sonic shaping of the whole that arises from their transformations and interplay. The model for such analysis is to be found in linguistic phonology (the science of language sounds), for in language too, sounds (bundles of sonic features) are shaped in order to present certain relations, functions, and values that, finally, distinguish or bear meanings.[4]

So we shall analyze the constituent spectral elements of each particular sonic moment of the *Ensembles*, in the portion of it we are examining. We shall also consider the interrelationships of each of these moments; and finally, try to define the particular sound shape to which they all ultimately contribute. We do so with the awareness that a composer, in composing, creates a sonic entity, a sound shape, which is most often a characteristic, perhaps uniquely intimate and personal, sonic formation that we can now approach, analyze, and define. This is so in virtually all music, but especially so in electronic music where the fundamental premise is creation by the composer, through the synthesizer (or through the computer acting as synthesizer), of all of a music's sounds and sound formations or sonic relationships.

II An Informal View

The beginning of Babbitt's *Ensembles*: four separate predominating sonic pillars, each lasting nine seconds, and each a distinctly conceived sonority (Fig. 1: a, b, c, and d).[5] By their inner complexity as well as by their distinctive conception, one from the other, these pillar-like sound complexes challenge our ability to understand and describe sonic likenesses and differences. With sonorities of such profile and character, it would certainly seem that means must already exist for their description, analysis, and understanding, even though these are not the off-the-shelf geometric wave forms or instrumental analogs of much electronic composition.

But it is exactly here, although not only here, that we directly confront the lacuna in our inherited theories already mentioned above. Just as we have lacked means for describing the distinguishing vocal nuances of Tibetan chant or for the striking sonorities of Japanese court (Gagaku) or shakuhachi instrumental music, for the instrumental and vocal sounds of Bach (whether on appropriate or inappropriate instruments), Berlioz, Debussy, or Stravinsky, and for the sonic forms

60

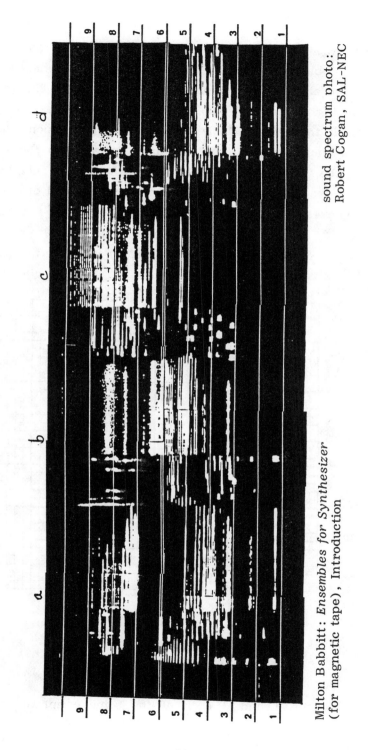

Milton Babbitt: *Ensembles for Synthesizer*
(for magnetic tape), Introduction

sound spectrum photo:
Robert Cogan, SAL-NEC

61

(diverse or alike) these musics all create, so too do we lack them for Babbitt's precisely synthesized pillars. What are the effective, affecting elements of each sonic complex? The special, distinguishing characteristics of each? Taken as a sonic ensemble, is there a particular sense to their succession? How do they, and their immediate surroundings, manage to foreshadow and imply the full sonic world of the *Ensembles*?

In Figure 2 a somewhat simplified spectral model of the four sonic complexes is derived from Figure 1:

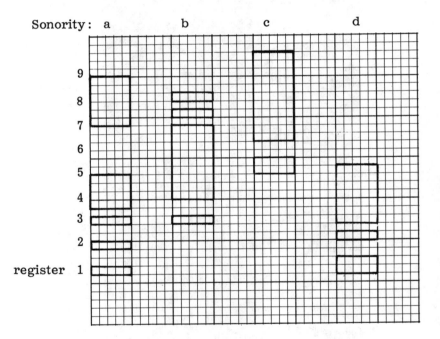

In both Figures 1 and 2 each of the sonic complexes clearly

reveals a unique registration.[6] In the sonic analysis we continually observe the importance of the intrinsic registral colorations first posited by Mach. Each spectral element that is present in a given register of a sonority injects into that sonority the specific sonic quality, or value, of that particular register. In the Babbitt passage each sonority is a unique selection and combination of registral colors, a unique mixture of specific registral absences, presences, and saturations.

The registral colors are organized so that the ensemble of sonorities progresses toward the registral extremities that are realized in the last two sonorities. On the largest scale, sonorities a and b oppose sonorities c and d:

a and b are both registrally mixed (acute
plus grave registers), but are not focused
on the registral extremities;[7]
while c and d are both focused on the
registral extremities, but do not mix them.

In a and b the mixture of registral colors, grave and acute, is achieved in two different ways. In a it is highlighted by the wide space gap within the sonority: the almost complete emptiness of registers 5 and 6, which vividly separates the grave and acute elements and regions, registers 1-4 and 7-8, from each other. In sonority b, on the other hand, the mixture of qualities is accomplished by centering: by its intense activation of the neutral middle registers of the total context, registers 4-6, as opposed to its more sparse, brief, and faint activation of acute and grave elements in registers 3, 7, and 8.

By contrast, in sonorities c and d the opposing colors, grave and acute, are isolated from each other rather than mixed: c focuses entirely on the acute region, especially registers 6-9, activating the most acute register, register 9, for the first time in the piece; while sonority d concentrates exclusively on the comparatively grave region, registers 1-4, displaying the

63

greatest saturation of grave registers, registers 1 and 3, so far in the piece.

So while in the largest view the sonority pairs are opposed, ab/cd, the individual members of each sonority pair are also vividly opposed a/b and c/d. Or most concisely:

a/b / c/d

The specific, unalterable register deployment and consequent register color of each sonority are clear, as is the role of each sonic complex in the unfolding succession. The role of sonority b is especially interesting. It draws the spectral focus toward the neutral center just prior to the outward expansion to the widest extremities in c and d. This serves to heighten c and d, which saturate the spectral extremities, but which also reach their opposing extremities, acute and grave, by flaring out from b at the spectral center.

Taken together, these four introductory sonic pillars open up virtually the entire human audible range, registers 1-9, while drawing from it in the four sonorities a striking variety of mixed and pure, extreme and centered, acute and grave colorations.[8] From its own specific spectral deployment, as well as from its systematic opposition to the other sonorities, each of the four complexes acquires its sharp profile and color, just as the entire passage reveals its inevitable cohesion and direction.

And what of the inner formation of each sonority? As we have already noticed, each of the spectra is individually conceived and synthesized. They are not the conventional strands, more or less widely spread, of vocal or instrumental harmonic spectra; nor are they, for the most part, conventionally full or randomly packed bands of noise.[9] Rather, each sonority is a uniquely formed agglomerate, or web, of more or less closely stacked spectral strands. The agglomerates are constructed so as to saturate chosen spectral regions. They often reinforce the presentation of these regions by staggered resoundings at various speeds of their elements, as shown by the speckles, dots, and dashes covering certain areas of the spectrum photo (see Figure 1, sonority b, registers 4, 5, and 6; sonority c, registers 7, 8, and 9).

At the same time, as we have already observed, space gaps (like holes in the sculptures of Henry Moore) play a formative role in all of the sonorities. In a, the large gap in the middle separates the strongly opposed grave and acute regions from each other. In b, two gaps, in register 3 and in registers 6-7, isolate the weaker spectral elements at the extremities from the more pronounced neutral, middle register agglomerate that dominates the sonic complex. In the acute complex, c, the gap in registers 5-6 separates the less acute elements (register 5) from the more extreme acute agglomerate (in registers 6-9) that dominates and characterizes the sonority.

Taken together the two complementary processes of spectral saturation and spectral spacing (by gaps) combine with specific registral placement to forge the characteristic sonic profile of each of the four complexes. Each sonority is a distictively shaped and weighted barrage of spectral impulses from its chosen region(s).

The Spectrum Photo, Figure 1, reveals, as well, that the sonorities all display a characteristic spectral shaping in time that further complements their shaping in space. Each sonority, as it approaches its conclusion, thins out. Each sonority, however, does this in a way that retains and intensifies its own particular sonic characteristic. For example, in sonority a, characterized by its mixture of registers ranging from grave to acute, elements in all of its diverse regions (registers 1, 3, 4, and 7) continue and remain intermixed to its very end, even as many spectral details disappear. In contrast, in the centered sonority, b, it is the central registers (registers 4 and 6) that prevail to the end, while the non-essential extremities (registers 3 and 6-8) thin out and disappear. Likewise, in the extreme acute sonority, c, the most extreme acute registers (registers 8-9) are the ones that continue to the end.

Just as each sonority occupies a specific spatial locus and is modeled by areas of spectral saturation and open spacing to create for each of them a sharply defined sonic quality, so too does their spectral modeling in time keep the same particular sonic quality of each in clear focus, even as each sonority thins out. In other words each sonority, as it unfolds in time, presents more, and then less, dense variants of the same registral coloration.

In its spectral space-time formation the section's concluding sonority, d, is shaped somewhat differently from the three spectral complexes that precede it. At its onset (Figure 1, just prior to d) can be seen and heard a brief moment of flickering activity in the acute spectral region (registers 6-8) that contrasts sharply with the otherwise predominant grave spectral elements (registers 1-3) of this generally dark-hued sonority. The momentary acute spectral elements recall the presence of those registers in each of the preceding complexes (sonorities a, b, and c). The brief, intense mixture of grave and acute features, separated by interior gaps, especially echoes sonority a, the originating sonority of the progression. The subsequent thinning out of sonority d, with its prolongation of the neutral registers (registers 3-5), serves to recall those registers in sonorities a and, especially, b. Consequently, for an instant before it settles into its own grave spectral coloration, and again in its ultimate thinning out, sonority d recalls and ties together the entire succession of spectral colors.

The entire passage reveals a sonic shape of accumulating oppositions in which each uniquely crafted and conceived sonority and each sonic transformation plays an essential role. The details of each sonic complex are shaped in space and time, in ways that reinforce the sense of the whole passage, and that

66

bind its elements into a coherent, self-reflecting whole.

III A Formal View

As we have just seen, the structure of the introductory section is shaped by four opposing sonorities, each sonority being characterized by choices made from several pairs of opposing properties: acute/grave, mixed/pure, extreme/centered, dense/sparse. In other writings I have already shown how the oppositional analysis of sonorities can be extended and formalized in Tables of Oppositions, modeled after those used in linguistic phonology.[10]

On the following page appears a Table of Oppositions in which Babbitt's four sonic complexes are characterized in the vertical columns a-d. It is important to realize that any sonic moment represents not a single sonic property, but rather a bundle of choices from a whole set of sonic possibilities. Comparably, in linguistics a phoneme (the smallest independent linguistic unit) has been designated "a set, bundle, totality of concurrent sound properties."[11] The intrinsic complexity of linguistic sounds is possibly even more characteristic of musical sounds. The Table of Oppositions embodies thirteen opposing characteristics by which every musical sound distinguishes itself in its context: characteristics of spectral placement and scope, dynamics, envelope, tone modulation, and interference phenomena. Such a Table reveals how each moment is characterized by its particular choices from the entire repertoire of available sonic features. It allows us to comprehensively define and compare the sonic morphologies of any chosen moments in the piece.

In each of Babbitt's sonorities (or in those of any other musical context) each of the thirteen oppositions can be represented by its negative (-) or positive (+) pole; by a mixture of them (-+); or by an intermediate, neutral state (∅).

Table of Oppositions:
Babbitt, *Ensembles for Synthesizer*, Introduction

- +	a	b	c	d
grave/acute	-+	-+	+	-
centered/extreme	+	-	+	+
narrow/wide	+	+	-	-
compact/diffuse	-+	-+	-+	-
non-spaced/spaced	+	-	-	-
sparse/rich	+	+	+	+
soft/loud	ø	ø	ø	ø
level/oblique	-	-	-	-
steady/wavering	-	-	-	-
no-attack/attack	-	-	-	-
sustained/clipped	-+	-+	-+	-
beatless/beating	+	+	+	+
slow beats/fast beats	-+	-+	+	-
Neutral (ø)	1	1	1	1
Negative (-)	3	5	5	9
Mixed (-+)	4	4	2	0
Positive (+)	5	3	5	3

Totals	(-7	(-9	(-7	(-9
	+9)	+7)	+7)	+3)
	+2	-2	0	-6

Totals:
a b c d

Non-variables (——) = 6   Variables = 7

a:b 2 change/5 constant   a:c 4/3   a:d 6/1
                            b:c 4/3   b:d 6/1
                                       c:d 4/3

Ratio of Change:
.29 (2/7)   .57 (8/14)   .76 (16/21)
  at b   at c   at d

68

The negative forms are low energy states: low spectral frequency, low intensity, low activity, low internal contrast. The positive forms are high energy states: high spectral frequency, high intensity, high activity, high internal contrast. For example, registrally grave (lower frequency) is negative, while acute (higher frequency) is positive. Narrow spectrum (low internal contrast) is negative, wide (high internal contrast) is positive. In density, sparse is negative, rich positive; and so forth. For its thirteen distinct sonic features the Table records the positive or negative orientation of each sonority. In this way, negative and positive themselves assume the role of meta-features. At the base of each column of the Table are found totals of the negative and positive features of each sonority, and a Totals line that summarizes the negative and positive orientation of each sonic moment.

The table is constructed so as to include within its organizing framework all spectral distributions and the full panorama of available tone color characteristics. A composer makes choices among the opposing features which chisel away certain of the total (and contradictory) possibilities of the sonic medium, revealing in the end the specific morphology of each sonority and the sound shape of each context.
The significance of these choices can be seen by comparing sonorities and contexts.

This comparison of sonorities and contexts can take several forms. Since, in the Spectrum Photo (Figure 1) and in Part II of this chapter ("An Informal View") we have already shown and considered the specific spectral formations of the sonorities, we will leave the detailed choices among oppositions and their detailed comparison aside in order to show here larger-scale sonic comparisons.

First among these, let us observe that Babbitt's four sonorities move steadily from dominance of the positive to dominance of the negative pole. This progression can be observed in two interrelated ways:

the growth of purely negative features: -3, -5, -5, -9;

the changing relative balance between negative and positive features in the Totals: a, (-7, +9), +2; b, (-9, +7), -2; c, (-7, +7), 0; d, (-9, +3), -6. (See the graph on the Table of Oppositions).

In Part II ("An Informal View") we already observed that the four sonorities form a directed spectral flow as they progress from mixed-register spectral distributions to focus on the registral extremities, first high and then low, a progression now summarized in the grave/acute line of the Table: -+, -+, +, -. In the Table of Oppositions we now observe that almost every sonic characteristic progresses to its negative pole in the final sonority, while simultaneously the positive characteristics diminish toward zero. Consequently, the sonic transformation to grave registers (negative) is amplified by the numerous parallel transformations to negative forms in almost every sonic feature of the last sonority. The structural evolution of the progression can most inclusively be described not simply by its registral transformations, as telling as those are, but rather by the entire coordinated set of transformations to negative sonic characteristics at its close.

We see in this instance that analysis of the sonic features in terms of negative and positive reveals how an entire context shapes itself; how the Babbitt introduction displays a two-step progression from positive (+2) to negative (-6) over intermediate sonorities (-2 and 0). This progressive transformation emerges especially vividly in the graph accompanying the Table of Oppositions.

In the Spectrum Photo (Figure 3) and the Table of

70

Oppositions on the following pages, the climax of Alban Berg's opera *Wozzeck* (Act III, Scene 2, mm. 109 ff.), a contrasting example can be observed. Its first phrase, the first half of the Spectrum Photo (Figure 3), progresses from overwhelming negative to overwhelming positive sonic character:

$$(-12, +0) \qquad (-2, +12)$$
$$-12 \longrightarrow +10$$

(where -+13 is the ultimate limit in either direction)[12]
In this phrase, heretofore always regarded as the very prototype of the static, the sonic moments at the beginning and end reveal a strikingly complete sonic reversal! While in the same phrase the middle, -2 (-8, +6), stands at the almost exact symmetrical midpoint between extremities![13] Far from being static, the phrase emerges as a profoundly shaped, directed, and coordinated set of transformations.

In contrast to Babbitt's sound shape, positive $\longrightarrow$ negative, Berg's progresses negative $\longrightarrow$ positive. The transformational processes work equally freely in both directions, which is a source of great potential richness and variety.[14]

The table of oppositions, then, offers a way of defining the many available finely detailed features that comprise sonic character. At the same time it offers a model of how whole sets of sonic characteristics combine and work together; and especially, how they do so to create sensations of direction of sonic transformation, negative or positive.

In evaluating a sonic context, the process of change itself, for example its speed and distance, can be as revealing as the direction of change, negative or positive. The process of change is revealed, in part, by the Ratio of Change, traced at the bottom of the Babbitt Table of Oppositions.

The Ratio of Change is calculated by comparing the exact morphology of each sonic moment, in terms of each feature, with the morphology of every previous sonic moment. In doing so it

71

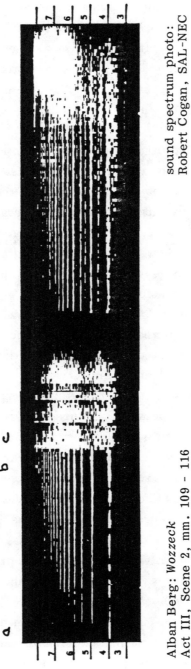

Alban Berg: *Wozzeck*
Act III, Scene 2, mm. 109 - 116

sound spectrum photo:
Robert Cogan, SAL-NEC

Table of Oppositions:

Berg, *Wozzeck*, Act III, Scene 2, mm. 109 - 116

- +	a	b	c
grave/acute	-	-+	-+
centered/extreme	-	+	+
narrow/wide	-	+	+
compact/diffuse	-	-	+
non-spaced/spaced	-	-	-
sparse/rich	-	+	+
soft/loud	-	+	+
level/oblique	-	-	+
steady/wavering	-	-	+
no-attack/attack	-	-	+
sustained/clipped	-	-	+
beatless/beating	-	+	+
slow beats/fast beats	∅	-	+

	a	b	c
Neutral (∅)	1	0	0
Negative (-)	12	7	1
Mixed (-+)	0	1	1
Positive (+)	0	5	11

Totals	(-12	(-8	(-2
	0)	+6)	+12)
	-12	-2	+10

Totals
a b c

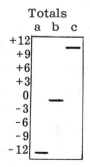

73

emerges that the process of change has several aspects. There is, for example, local change: constancy (or contrast) between each feature in adjacent sonorities. And there is global change: constancy (or contrast) between each feature in all the previous sonorities, adjacent and distant, which involves not only the comparison of distant points, but also shows the results of the entire accumulating process of change.

The Change calculations on the Table first compare every feature of every sonority with every feature of every previous sonority for constancy of change. In terms of local constancy and change, the adjacent sonorities of Babbitt's progression show a gradually increasing quantity of change:

```
change    2    4    4
constant  5    3    3
          a:b  b:c  c:d
```

(These measurements take only the seven variable features of the context into account; the six non-variables in Babbitt's context play no part in these calculations. This is consistent with the linguistic principle of contextual determination of features: the constants are never factors of change.)

At the same time the calculations reveal that the transformations carry the sonic character even further away from the quality of the first sonority. This is seen by comparing sonority a with each succeeding sonority:

```
change    2    4    6
constant  5    3    1
          a:b  a:c  a:d
```

The Ratio of Change shown below the specific fractional comparisons of constancy and change on the Table of Oppositions is a calculation of the total quantity (and total quality) of change represented by any sonic moment compared to all that has preceded it. As has been indicated, it is figured by comparing all features of all the previous sonorities with which

74

any point can be compared, near and far. This global change might, consequently, be regarded as an index of overall sonic "freshness" in a given context. In the Babbitt introduction, the Ratios of Change indicate how special the last sonority is in comparison to the sonorities that precede it. The last sonority displays by far the highest Ratio of change, .76, compared with .29 and .57 for the preceding sonorities. Not only is the last sonority the most distant from the first sonority in sonic characteristics (6 features changed, only 1 constant): it is also reached by an accelerating momentum of sonic change, represented by the soaring Ratio of Change. We might well note that to maintain an increasing Ratio of Change in an evolving context, and thereby increasing (rather that decreasing) sonic freshness, is neither a common nor a trivial compositional accomplishment. This increasing Ratio of Change sums up, by taking all of the sonic features and transformations of the phrase into account, all of the changes of sonic quality (direction and distance together) in the introduction of Babbitt's *Ensembles*.

The Table of Oppositions has made possible, then, wholly new insights into the total formation of Babbitt's context. These include the realization that it is shaped by a single overriding direction of sonic transformation, positive ⟶ negative. And by measureable amounts of sonic change as the passage unfolds: gradually increasing local change from one sonority to the next; but especially, continually accumulating and intensifying global change as the progression moves from its beginning to its end. Sonic processes previously unrecognizable and undefinable emerge as precisely and intricately shaped.

IV Conclusion

The shaping and understanding of such sonic formations - in which each individual sonority, as well as their ensemble, is an authentic creation - poses if not a wholly new challenge then at least, a new intensification of an old challenge. To sense the particular quality of each sonority, and to understand the role of each in the unfolding sonic formation of Babbitt's introduction, has required two intense, concentrated views of it: the one informal, the other formal. Both views relate to two distinct scientific analytical disciplines: spectrum analysis, as practiced in many domains of physics including the acoustical; and building upon that, the analysis of the functions, relations, and values of the special features, as well as of the other distinctive sonic elements and features in a sonic context, as developed in structural linguistics (phonology).

In this way we arrive at a clear view of shaped structures formed by sounds themselves. At this level, the instrumental (or "motor") production of the sounds recedes in importance, while their qualitative, structure-building powers grow in importance. Here too, structural linguistics has pointed out the essential truths:

"The impression produced on the ear is the natural basis of all theory" (Saussure).

"It is not the movements of the speech organs but the speech sounds themselves which are primary in language" (Thomson).[15]

Ultimately, it hardly matters whether the source of a sound formation is a bassoon, a bongo drum, a brain wave, or Babbitt's Columbia-Princeton based synthesizer. The instrument is a means, however useful, however distinctive, to an end. That end is the formation of sonic moments: sonic moments engendering significant larger sonic formations, and taking their significance from those formations. Ultimately, it is not the romance of the synthesizer that we celebrate, but rather the shaping of Babbitt's sounds and sonic context.

The introduction of Babbitt's *Ensembles* provides an

instance of whole sets of sonic characteristics working together to create sensations of sonic direction (negative or positive), of sonic distance (the relative quantity of transformation), and of transformational momentum and freshness (the Ratio of Change). It is formed of authentic, individually shaped sonic complexes, to be understood and savored as such. They cannot be reduced: neither to single pitches, nor to single instrument or simple wave form analogs. Their perception needs, ultimately, to encompass and evaluate all of the many sonic facets of these vivid aural objects and experiences. They offer a basis for shaping and understanding an art formed of such sonic complexes. They, and other equally shaped sonic contexts, even announce that genuine rarity, a new stage of musical art. This may justify, if anything can, their extended consideration here, and to come.

1) Further information on the ideas presented in this paper may be found in Robert Cogan, *New Images of Musical Sound* (Harvard University Press, 1984)

2) See the following: Robert Cogan and Pozzi Escot, *Sonic Design: The Nature of Sound and Music* (Englewood Cliffs, New Jersey: Prentice Hall, 1976), Chapter 4, "The Color of Sound"; Robert Cogan, "Tone Color:The New Understanding," *Sonus* (Fall, 1980); and Robert Cogan, "Stravinsky's Sound, A Phonological View: Stravinsky the Progressive," *Sonus* (Spring, 1982).

3) This chapter uses analytical photos created with a sound spectrum analysis facility developed by Dr. Dale Teaney and Charles Potter at IBM's Watson Research Center, which, during the years 1980-81, was located in the Sonic Analysis Laboratory of the New England Conservatory of Music (SAL-NEC). The photos were taken by the author of this article. In musical instrument and vocal sounds we often think of sound spectrum as the fundamental pitch plus all sounding partials (overtones). However, the reader should keep in mind that in electronically synthesized music the composer composes all of the sonic elements, "fundamentals" (where they appear) and other "partials" alike. The distinction between them falls away: they are all spectral elements alike. Spectrum photos such as those shown here are ways, then, of notating the essential contents of such composition.

4) See Cogan, "Stravinsky's Sound...", *op cit.*

5) Milton Babbitt, *Ensembles for Synthesizer*, Columbia Record MS-7051. Prof. Wayne Slawson first pointed out some of the significance of this passage from Babbitt's composition in a paper delivered to the Society for Music Theory in Denver, November 1980; and again at the Eastman School of Music, February, 1981. I am greatly indebted to him for bringing it to my attention on those occasions and for stimulating my interest in it. (Also, see note 9).

6) On the spectrum photos and graphs, and in the text, registers are numbered as recommended by the International Acoustical Convention. Each register begins on C and ascends through B: for reference, $C1 = 33$ Hz, $C4 = 262$ Hz (middle C), and $C8 = 4186$ Hz.

7) The terms grave and acute, describing the opposition of the lowest and highest spectral regions, are adopted from linguistic phonology. Roman Jakobson and Linda Waugh, *The Sound Shape of Language* (Bloomington, Indiana: Indiana University Press, 1979), pp. 92 - 95. Also, Roman Jakobson, C. Gunnar, M. Fant, and M. Halle, *Preliminaries to Speech Analysis* (Cambridge, Massachusetts: MIT Press, 1976), pp. 29 - 30.

8) Conventionally, 20,000 Hz (20 kHz) is regarded as the upper limit of the human audible range. Since register 10 stretches from ca. 16 - 33 kHz, it almost entirely exceeds the limit. Register 9 is, consequently, the highest complete register in the human audible range. In sonority c, Babbitt covers it completely.

9) In his paper Slawson suggests understanding these sonorities as specific vowel analogs, rather than as wave-form or musical instrument analogs. While his is undoubtedly an improvement on the wave-form or musical instrument model, his specific vowel model, too, introduces unnecessary, undesirable bias, limitations, and inaccuracies into the sonic analysis. For example, sonority c would be considered an i (ee) analog. However, an exact i analog would have its lowest principal resonances (low formant, or F1) in register 4, rather than in register 5 where they appear in Babbitt's sonority. Furthermore, the i analog offers no basis for understanding the intense concentration of partials in registers 8 and 9, which is contextually the most novel and striking element of Babbitt's sonority. We want, ideally, to understand sonorities such as these in their own terms: as unique sounds, with unique contextual functions. Even Slawson's specific vowel model represents a potential impoverishment, by limiting our understanding to the spectral range and features of human voices and specific linguistic sounds. This should not be confused with our own presentation of a general oppositional model below (and elsewhere), which redefines linguistic structural features of musical sounds and contexts (see III, "A Formal View").

10) Cogan, "Stravinsky's Sound,,,", op.cit. pp. 18 - 20; and Cogan, New Images of Musical Sound (Harvard University Press, 1984). Also see Jakobson, Gunnar, Fant, and Halle, op.cit., pp. 43 - 45.

11) Jakobson and Waugh, op. cit., p. 19.

12) Thirteen is the maximum because there exist (so far as we can see) thirteen pairs of opposing sonic features.

13) See the graph and the Berg Table of Oppositions.

14) Compare the unidirectional transformations found here with the oscillating transformations found in Stravinsky: Cogan, "Stravinsky's Sound...", op. cit., p. 20. The oscillating transformations represent yet another structural possibility,

15) Quoted in Jakobson and Waugh, op. cit., pp. 61 and 27 respectively.

Form and Process

Wesley York

Preface

Much controversy has surrounded the work of the American composer, Philip Glass. Although his compositions have been performed with critical and popular acclaim in Europe and America, in such auspicious institutions as Carnegie Hall and the Metropolitan Opera, there have been few efforts to understand the structure of this music and there seems to have been little, if any, serious analysis of the work to justify praise or criticism. Many questions remain to be asked:

- Is there any underlying structure creating and supporting the shapes we hear?
- Does the opening of the piece have any special significance in relation to the rest of the piece?
- What purpose does the process of repetition serve?
- What motivates the minimalist nature of this music?

This paper attempts to answer these and other crucial questions through a detailed analysis of Glass' *Two Pages* for electric organ and piano (1968) and perhaps throws some light on the larger body of works which the composer has produced since 1968.

As is true of many of his pieces, it becomes immediately apparent that Glass makes his statement through the shaping of a minimal number of musical materials. There are no dynamic changes, no new pitch materials after the initial five pulses, no changes of instrumentation, and no juxtapositions of sound and silence. Rather, and stated most simply, contexts of up to five pitches are continually shaped and re-shaped as they articulate an even and unchanging pulse. Ultimately, the structure of *Two Pages* can be understood as first, the exposition and juxtaposition of two sets of opposing processes, and then, the coordination of all shapes which both emerge from, and reflect back on, those processes. Thus, the emergence of formal relationships occurs through the interaction of the various processes themselves. Regarding this emerging form, it becomes apparent that the symmetrical arch shape pervades the entire piece.

A) Preliminary Considerations

Before proceeding to the analysis itself, a brief discussion is in order with respect to three important factors: first of all, terminology; second, the types of processes at work in the piece; and finally, the particular graphic-analytic method employed in the analysis. After these preliminaries, the structure of the piece will be discussed in some detail.

Reproduced on the following two pages is a transcription of the Shandar recording (#83515) of *Two Pages*.[1]

Terminology

The work is comprised of five parts. Each of these parts is subdivided into several sections:

Part I   - three sections
Part II - three sections
Part III - two sections

82

TWO PAGES by Philip Glass
transcription: Wesley York

84

Part IV - two sections

Part V - three sections

Each section, in turn, includes one or more measures and each measure contains a number of repetitions of a single melodic pattern. For example:

m. 1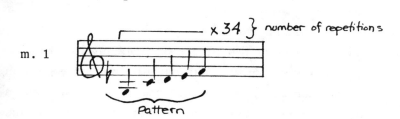

Once again, a measure includes the pattern with all of its repetitions.

Processes

With respect to the various processes at work, one finds two types which are responsible for creating all motion and change within the composition. One of these is a subtractive process; the other is additive.

The process involved in moving from pattern to pattern, shown in the example below, can be understood as a subtractive process. The five-note group becomes a four-note group by the subtraction of one note. This subtractive process will be referred to as process A.

mm. 1-2

The other process involved in moving from pattern to pattern is an additive one. In the example below, a five note pattern is expanded into six notes. This additive process will be referred

85

to as process B :

mm. 7-8

In addition, there are two processes involving repetition - external repetition and internal repetition. All external repetition involves the repetition of an entire pattern. As may be seen in measure 1, in such a case, the number of repetitions is external to the pattern. This procedure will be referred to as process Alpha:

m. 1

In contrast, internal repetition involves the repetition of only part of a pattern. As such, the number of repetitions is internal to the pattern. Measure 20, shown below, is an example of a pattern with such internal repetitions, which will be referred to as process Beta:[2]

m. 20

Finally, one should note that, at certain points, external repetitions are superimposed on a pattern with internal repetitions:

m. 15

The Graph

In Graph 1 on the following page, all measures of the composition are notated in terms of pulses (one pulse equals a quarter note in the transcription). Successive measures are plotted along the horizontal axis, numbers of pulses along the vertical axis. There are three lines shown. The broken line represents the number of pulses per pattern (without external repetitions). The dotted line shows the unfolding of the repetitions of process Alpha. Finally, the solid line connects points which represent the total number of pulses per measure: this is the number resulting from the multiplication of the number of pulses of a particular measure with the number of external repetitions of the pattern of that measure (process Alpha). The significance of Graph 1 will emerge in the analysis which follows.

B) Analysis

The following chart outlines the overall formal plan of Two Pages:

Part I

Section 1	Section 2	Section 3
mm. 1-3	mm. 4-6	m. 7

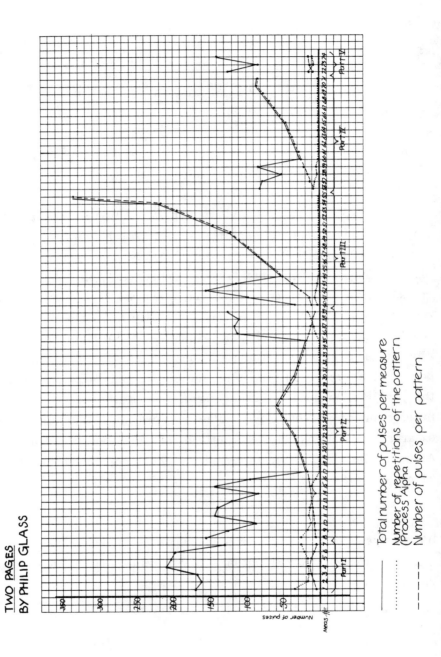

GRAPH 1
TWO PAGES
BY PHILIP GLASS

Total number of pulses per measure
Number of repetitions of the pattern
(Process Alpha)
Number of pulses per pattern

88

Part II

Section 1	Section 2	Section 3
mm. 8-16	mm. 17-35	mm. 36-39

Part III

Section 1	Section 2
mm. 40-43	mm. 44-55

Part IV

Section 1	Section 2
mm. 56-59	mm. 60-71

Part V

Section 1	Section 2	Section 3
m. 72	m. 73	m. 74

Part I (measures 1-7)

Part I consists of seven measures. In it the composer employs both processes A (subtraction) and Alpha (external repetition) which interact to expand those patterns and measures into three larger groups, to be called sections 1, 2, and 3. As was mentioned earlier, the motion from the pattern of measure 1 to the pattern of measure 2 provides the first example of process A. Process A is continued until measure 4, the midpoint of part I, where it reaches its furthest extrapolation:

Process A is then reversed through measures 5 and 6, and in measure 7 returns to the opening pattern. Thus, part I outlines an arch-shaped motion. (This is reflected in the symmetrical arch-shape seen in the broken line of Graph 1 which, as mentioned earlier, represents process A.) Process Alpha (the dotted line) then may be understood as superimposed onto the ongoing pattern-to-pattern motion of process A.

Next, it should be noted that the intersection of process A with process Alpha creates three groups of measures, three different plateaus each consisting of measures with a similar number of pulses (ca. 170, ca. 200, ca. 130) and, therefore, a similar duration. These three groups of measures will be referred to as sections 1, 2, and 3. Significantly, none of these sections is articulated by process A alone (the broken line) as process A is continuous and uninterrupted. Likewise, none of the sections is articulated by process Alpha alone (the dotted line) which is also a continuous unbroken progression lacking any internal subdivisions. It is, however, when these two processes are superimposed that the three sections of part I emerge with vivid clarity:

Solid Line
(Graph 1)

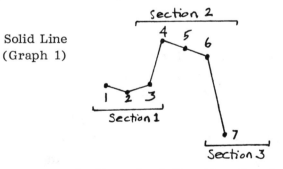

Closer examination of relationships found among the various parameters in part I shows the symmetrical relationship and the proportion 4:5 to be of primary importance. Significantly, in terms of the former, one may note that musical space itself is proportioned symmetrically. The five pitches are organized as two perfect fourths G-C and C-F), the first of which being a

90

leap and the second being filled in symmetrically. These five tones comprise the complete set of pitches for the entire piece and are exposed immediately as the pattern of measure 1:

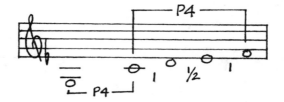

The symmetrical organization of pitches maintains an ambiguity as to which is the stressed tone. If, for example, the F were an F# - breaking the symmetry - a less ambiguous, and perhaps less interesting, situation would result. (Over the course of this analysis it will become clear that the concept of ambiguity is indeed central to the entire composition.)

The perfectly symmetrical arch of part I, unveiled by calculating the number of pulses per pattern has already been noted. However, there are also several symmetrical relationships to be found among the total number of pulses per measure (the solid line of Graph 1). As might have been expected, measure 4, the central measure, is the highest point on the curve. Comparing this central measure with the first and last measures of this first part, one finds that, in terms of duration, the point representing measure 1 is exactly midway between those points representing measures 4 and 7, respectively, the highest and lowest of part I:

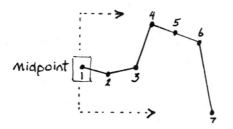

Such symmetry is not only apparent in the disposition of pitches employed, but is also apparent in the temporal structure of part I. As the following chart demonstrates, there exists a virtual symmetry, with respect to the total number of pulses around the central measure:

```
        r — — — — — — — 94% — — — — — — — — ┐
┌────────────────┐ ┌──────────────┐ ┌──────────────────┐
│measures 1,2,3  │ │measure 4     │ │measures 5,6,7    │
     500 pulses        210 pulses        532 pulses
└──────────────────────── Part I ─────────────────────────┘
```

In addition to such symmetrical relationships, the proportion 4:5 (80%) is reflected on several levels. Initially, it was noted that the pattern of measure 1 exposed a gesture of four step-wise notes inside a gesture of five notes. Following this, the pattern of measure 2 consists of a gesture of four notes following a gesture of five. In addition, the proportion of total pulses in measure 1 to total pulses in measure 4 is 4:5, as is the relationship of total pulses in measure 7 to those in measure 1. In fact, throughout part I the proportion 4:5 seems to permeate the arrangement of total pulses per measure:

```
      r — — 4:5 — — — — ┐
m. 1    m. 2   m. 3   m. 4   m. 5   m. 6   m. 7
          L — - 4:5 — ┘
        L — —  — - 4:5 — —  — ┘
   L — — — — — — 4:5 — — — — — ┘
```

In summary, the final shape of part I and the most significant proportions found therein are brought about through the interaction of process A and process Alpha. As we shall see, this mode of unfolding formal relationships is of central importance to the piece as a whole.

Part II (measures 8-39)

Part II is in three sections: section 1 (measures 8-16), section 2 (measures 17-35), and section 3 (measures 36-39). In it, a new process, additive, is introduced:

mm. 7-8

Each new measure from 7 to 15 adds one new note. Then from measures 16 through 22, each bar adds three new notes: F-D-Eb, which will be referred to as the "tag" of the pattern. From measures 23 through 26 two statements of this tag are added. Consequently, beginning at measure 8 there is a steady accumulation of pulses per pattern, until a climax is reached at measure 26, in which one finds a total of 58 pulses comprising one pattern.

After measure 26 the music proceeds essentially through a mirror image of what has just been described. Of course, this type of symmetrical motion was also observed in part I. In this instance, however, the listener is not brought back all the way to the initial pattern (i.e. to measure 8). The return, in contrast, arrives only at a reiteration of measure 9, which enables the composer to preserve the tag ending intact as part II concludes:

One point, however, should be clarified. On Graph 1, the arch shape of the line representing the number of pulses per pattern of part I was the result of process A. In contrast to this, in part II the similar arch-shape is the result of both process B and process Beta. It should be emphasized that process Beta evolves in part II as an intensification of process B, and that process Beta is, therefore, included on Graph 1 as contributing to this arch.

Next, it should be noted that process Alpha is also operative in part II. Referring to Graph 1, it may be observed that process Alpha (the dotted line) descends from measures 8 through 17. Then, from measures 17 through 35, there is only one statement of each pattern. Finally, from measures 36 through 39, the dotted line ascends. Thus, with respect to process Alpha one finds, for the first time, a long section in which there are no external repetitions. As will be shown, this shape, first exposed in part II, will recur in parts III and IV.

Referring now to the progression of total number of pulses per measure in part II, (represented by the solid line) it is obvious that, as in part I, the interaction of two quite continuous processes, B and Beta (represented by the broken line) with Alpha, (represented by the dotted line) results in the articulation of three distinct sections:

Section 1 - measures 8-16

Section 2 - measures 17-35

Section 3 - measures 36-39

Specifically, section 1 is characterized by the gradual formation of the tag; section 2, by the addition and subtraction of successive statements of the tag; and section 3, the gradual removal of all internal repetitions. Incidentally, the resulting concave shape of the solid line on Graph 1 occurs because of the absence of process Alpha in section 2.

It should be noted that it is in section 1 of part II, during the gradual formation of the tag, that we have the first hint of process Beta:

94

m. 12

Measure 12 contains the first multiple statement of the tag ending, F-D-Eb, and thus, the first instance of internal repetition.

One significant by-product of the additive process in part II is the gradual lessening of the stability associated with the notes G-C as established in part I. Concomitant with this increasing instability is the growing expectation for a return to the G-C as it is denied for longer and longer periods. The interesting corollary to this development, however, is the subtle but steady establishment of F-D-Eb as a more potent center unto itself. As such, there seems to be a growing sense of polarity between a G-C cell and an F-D-Eb cell.

Part III (measures 40-55)

Overview

Part III is in two sections: section 1 (measures 40-43) and section 2 (measures 44-55). Thus far in the piece, part I introduced processes A and Alpha, and part II introduced processes B and Beta. In contrast, part III combines all the processes from both previous parts in a *tour de force* which constitutes the central passage of the entire piece.

A brief examination of measure 43 will immediately reveal this combination of processes:

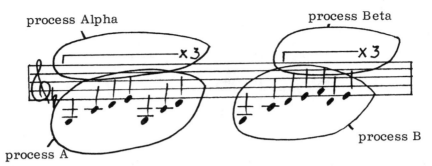

process Alpha

process Beta

process B

process A

Referring to the two patterns above, it is clear that the first half of the measure is borrowed from part I and, of course, represents a pattern from process A (subtractive). Opposing this, the music comprising the second half of this measure is borrowed from part II and represents a pattern from process B (additive).3 In addition, the entire seven note pattern which constitutes the first half of the measure is repeated three times, representing an example of process Alpha (external repetition). In contrast, in the second half of the measure, only part of the pattern is repeated. Thus, the repetition is here internal to the pattern and so represents an example of process Beta.

Referring now to Graph 1, a comparison of the above-mentioned pattern-to-pattern motion (broken line) of part III with those of parts I and II reveals a most significant difference. In parts I and II, the broken line rises, reaches a peak, and returns to, or quite near to, where it began. In contrast, the shape of part III rises to a peak, but then, instead of returning where it began, abruptly ends.

As was the case in parts I and II, in part III process Alpha is superimposed upon the pattern-to-pattern level referred to above. When the basically continuous evolution of processes A and Beta is combined with the similarly continuous motion of process Alpha, a rather dramatic division into two sections emerges (measures 40 through 43, and 44 through 55), illustrated in Graph 1 by the striking break in the solid line representing the total number of pulses per measure.

In summary, then, several important events take place in part III. Most significantly, there occurs a juxtaposition of the processes from part I with those of part II. In addition, the shape of the pattern-to-pattern motion, which described an arch in parts I and II, is quite different in part III. Finally, the superimposition of processes articulates two distinct sections.

A Closer Look at Part III

The logic of the first pattern of part III is impressive. The pattern holds within itself not only the continuation of the process from part II but also the seed from which part III grows:

mm. 39-40

As can be seen in the above example, the first four notes of measure 40 could represent a continuation of the process concluding in part II as it removes three more notes, the tag, from the previous pattern.

Indeed, the pattern of measure 40 represents, in microcosm, all of what is to come in part III. Every measure which succeeds it bears the same basic internal structure:

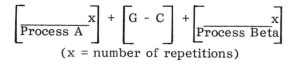
(x = number of repetitions)

The pattern of measure 42, for instance, is created by superimposing process Beta onto the pattern of measure 41. A subtle junction is thus made between the gestures labeled A and B, below. A question arises. Does one hear:

97

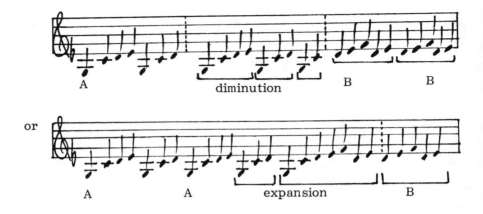

The answer, of course, is that one can hear either or both. The middle G-C can be understood as the end of a subtractive process or as the initiation of the process of building the new tag. The pattern of measure 43, however, clarifies the ambiguity, as it here becomes clear that the true structure consists of, first, repeating the seven-note gesture and then, adding five-note tags to G-C:

Process A with Alpha
-disjunct
-emphasis on G

Process Beta
-conjunct
-emphasis on D

In attempting to integrate these two gestures, the listener might perceive an element of instability in the first half of the measure in that there is no F. As such, when the note F occurs in the second half of the measure, there is a certain sense of completion. However, an unstable quality then seems to develop in the second half of the measure, by the complementary absence of G which is resolved when the G is heard again in the first half of the next measure.

Process Beta now unfolds as it did in part II - adding, at first, one more internal repetition per pattern, and then, eventually, two internal repetitions. Once again, however, unlike parts I and II, part III is not constructed as an arch-shape. As can be seen in Graph 1, part III ends at the furthest working out of its processes.

Curiously, as a result of the extensive simultaneous development of the two processes of part III, one senses a certain separation between the two halves of each measure:

In addition, along with this separation, a certain sense of expectation develops. With the continued repetition of the tag (in which D is the central pitch), one awaits the return of the seven-note gesture (in which G is the central pitch).

It must also be noted that the final measure of part III adds 19 extra internal repetitions of the tag, creating an added sense of expectation for a new event - the return of the note G. As we shall see, in the next measure (the first of part IV), this expectation is denied. Significantly, the number of pulses in measure 55 is the highest of the entire piece. It is interesting, too, that process Alpha (external repetition) is not involved in this central passage of the piece. It is the juxtaposition of processes on the more fundamental pattern-to-pattern level of form which articulates this focal point.

Part IV (measures 56 - 71)

Part IV contains two sections: section 1 (measures 56-59) and section 2 (measures 60-71). The most significant aspect of part IV is that it consists primarily of process Beta reversed. One might recall that Beta is that process which involves adding internal repetitions at the end of the pattern. Now, in part IV, the internal repetitions occur at the beginning of the pattern, as can be seen in the example below:

m. 57

Thus, the pattern-to-pattern evolution of part IV involves successive additions of the first gesture, while the second gesture remains constant. Specifically, in each succeeding pattern of part IV, one more internal repetition is added until a total of ten repetitions is reached. At this point, two internal repetitions are added per measure until twenty repetitions are reached. This basic motion would seem to duplicate that heard in parts II and III. However, it is significant to note that this motion does not mirror back on itself as it did in parts I and II. Rather, it recalls more the motion of part III since it also reaches a point of furthest extrapolation and then ends.

Referring to the pattern-to-pattern motion of this fourth part (the broken line of part IV on Graph 1), one finds a shape similar to that of part III: the continuous working out of the single process at hand. Although this process (shown by the broken line) begins at about the same number of pulses for both parts III and IV, in part III it rises to 336 pulses in the same number of measures in which in part IV it rises only to 85 pulses. In other words, the process in part IV is evolving at a much faster pace since its 16 measures unfold more rapidly (i.e.

100

contain many fewer pulses) than do those of part III. Thus, because of the more rapid evolution after the dramatic central passage of the piece, one might begin to feel a certain compelling force moving toward the completion of the composition.

In addition, process Alpha operates in part IV. The presence of external repetitions in the first four measures retards the movement of the pattern-to-pattern process. The use of such repetitions only in the first four measures helps create two sections. As has been mentioned, section 1 begins at measure 56, and section 2 at measure 60. Curiously, as in part III, the very last measure contains some extra repetitions. However, these serve a very different purpose than the final repetitions in part III, where the repetition of D-Eb-F-D-Eb builds expectation for a return to the note G. In contrast, the repetitions of C-D-Eb-F at the end of part IV give the central note C more weight. Supporting this is the fact that C is now the lowest tone of the pattern. It might be added, however, that although the note C acquires local emphasis, the pitch layout of measure 71 is, once again, symmetrical and, therefore, still basically ambiguous.

One final point: looking again at the pattern-to-pattern motion (the broken line) on Graph 1 and comparing the connections between each part, one sees a minor change of direction in the line between parts I and II, and between parts II and III. But, in contrast to this, between parts III and IV there is a leap which spans practically the entire depth of the graph. Significantly, this dramatic leap in the number of pulses per pattern is accompanied, as previously mentioned, by a denial of the expectation of the return to the note G.

Part V (measures 72-74)

Part V consists of the final three measures of the piece and, as we shall see, is comprised of three sections - each measure, in this case, being one section. Thus, in part V each

101

point on the solid line of Graph 1 seems like a small plateau unto itself. Indeed, the difference between each successive point on the resultant line of part V is equal to or greater than the distance which creates sections 1 and 2 in part I, thus enabling one to perceive a formal articulation.

Primarily, part V consists of process A inverted. Previously, process A always involved successive subtractions of one note from the top of the basic pattern. Contrasting with this, in part V these successive subtractions are taken from the bottom:

m. 74

Part V seems to recall many ideas from the first part of the score. In fact, the three patterns which comprise part V are directly analogous to those from measures 2, 3, and 4 of part I, although, as mentioned above, process A is now inverted. Specifically, as with the first part, the line representing the pattern-to-pattern process (broken line) in part V seems part of a convex arch, while the line representing process Alpha seems part of a concave formation. Indeed, the resultant line (solid) is basically an inversion of the general convex shape of that of part I, as the processes of parts I and V are both inversions of one another. Moreover, shapes from several other previous parts seem to be in evidence in part V. Referring to Graph 1, it may be noted that the pattern-to-pattern evolution of part V unfolds in a manner which is quite similar to parts III and IV since there is no mirror return.

Finally, in reference to repetition processes, as in part I, only process Alpha is operative here. There are, however, fewer external repetitions in part V than in part I, with the result that the measures of part V progress much faster than the analogous measures of the opening.

The Piece as a Whole

With the foregoing information, the essential characteristics of the entire five-part form may now be revealed. First of all, considering the total number of pulses in the entire piece (its duration), the midpoint of the work occurs in the very last measure of part II (measure 39). It may be recalled that the first two parts were expository in nature. As such, the piece divides precisely in half between exposition of materials and their further working out.

In contrast to this bipartite plan is the inherent symmetry of the composition's five-part scheme:

Part I	Part II	Part III	Part IV	Part V
Process A	Process B; Process Beta	Process A; Process Beta	Process Beta (as intensi- fication of B) reversed	Process A inverted

Understood in these terms, the work seems to articulate a tripartite form in which parts I and II function as exposition, part III as development, and parts IV and V as a varied return. Turning once more to Graph 1, it becomes immediately apparent that this symmetrical, ternary form is also reflected in the succession of arches which constitute the overall shape of each individual part:

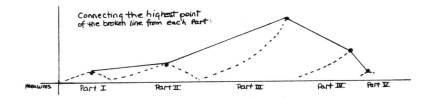

The chart on the following page represents an encapsulation of the entire analysis.

In summary, one discovers in *Two Pages* a compelling compositional framework. The piece concerns itself not with one single process, but with the interaction of several processes. In this interaction, ambiguities of several kinds act to propel the working out of the various processes toward the ultimate resolution. Together, these factors provide for one listener a rich aural experience.

	Exposition		Juxtaposition	Varied Return	
	Part I	Part II	Part III	Part IV	Part V
1) Pattern-to-Pattern Process:	Process A - subtracting from the top	Process B - adding to the end, beginning is static	Process A - with Process Beta	Process Beta - reversed	Process A - inverted, subtracting from the bottom
2) Type of Repetitive Process:	Process Alpha - external repetitions	Process Beta - internal repetitions	Processes Alpha and Beta	Processes Alpha and Beta	Process Alpha
3) Shape of Entire Part - solid line, Graph 1:	arch a — Process moves faster at ends	inverted arch b — Process moves slower at ends	$a + b$ — new shape	b — extension	$b + a^-$ — extension
4) Shape of Pattern-to-Pattern Process - broken line, Graph 1:	arches	arches	extends	extends	extends
5) Note given emphasis -	G (C also has some weight)	D	G and D juxtaposed as opposing centers	C	F

1) In conversation (January, 1980), Mr. Glass has mentioned that his score, as originally conceived, included two measures which were removed from the Shandar recording. These two measures, 23 and 24, were interpolated into the transcription of the recorded performance. Moreover, there may be further differences between the original score and the piece as represented by the Shandar recording. However, since, as of this writing, the score is not available, Mr. Glass has agreed to a reprinting of the present transcription.

2) Process Beta might well have been called process B^1 since it is introduced in part II as an intensification of process B, and also (and more importantly), it always functions in the same manner as processes A and B. However, since it is heard, I believe, as a repetition, we will identify it as process Beta.

3) It is important to note, however, that process B is not actually operative here, although, as shown in the second pattern of measure 43, it is explicitly quoted.

4) Ambiguities already discussed include the symmetrical layout of pitches as well as ambiguity in the flow of gestures (for example: Is measure 2 heard as five pulses followed by four or the reverse?). Further, the mechanical evenness of attack maintained by the organ heightens the sense of ambiguity. Finally, line 5 of the chart on the last page ("Note Given Emphasis") shows that emphasis rotates to every note except Eb. The composer thus avoids the only tone with a half-step (leading tone) below itself, thereby assuring ambiguity in terms of "tonal" orientation.

Part Two

Sound, Gesture and Symbol

Thomas DeLio

The radical nature of many of the new notational systems employed in the music of the '60's and the '70's lends particular insight into the character of their unique aural results. With respect to much of this recent music, a study of the notation employed can often supply valuable insight into many of the fundamental premises upon which a composition's structure rests. As attitudes toward materials and morphology change, it has become imperative that composers seek new methods by which their works may be notated, thereby enabling the accurate and detailed modeling of many revolutionary concepts of structure. Indeed, it has become apparent that "very often the notations themselves are the determining factors in the composition of a piece and hence the piece's identity and structure."[1]

The multifarious outpouring of new notational schemes in recent years is, of course, only a reflection of the amazing diversity of recent compositional practice. In fact, much of the impetus for recent exploration in the area of notation stems from the ongoing re-evaluation of our most basic notions of structure and the particular problems in charting, symbolically, the innovations which this re-evaluation engenders. Specifically, with respect to a great deal of new music one finds that activities which were once viewed as pre-compositional and outside the realm of structure are now being integrated directly into a composition's framework. The very concept of musical notation has been extended, then, to include not only the symbolic representation of form but also the delineation of all the compositional methodology from which such form issues.

More and more the composer finds himself facing the problem of notating the activities of composition, rather than any specific sonic results. It is this concern which links the notations of such diverse works as Iannis Xenakis' *Linaia-Agon* (1972), John Cage's *Cartridge Music* (1960), and Karlheinz Stockhausen's *Spiral* (1968). In each of these works, the activities of making and shaping are externalized, in some way, and integrated into the very notation of the composition.

Two attitudes toward notation will be discussed here, each of which reveals a very different vision of musical structure as reflected in the nature of the activities symbolized in the scores. The first deals with an exploration of the relationships between the structure of an artwork and the patterns of human behavior. This attitude is exemplified in those seminal works of Christian Wolff written throughout the '60's and many works of Robert Ashley. The second attitude deals with various notions of pluralism, as exemplified in many works of John Cage and the recent works of Pozzi Escot.

I) Behavior

One of the most striking aspects of Christian Wolff's music, and one of the central issues guiding the development of his innovative notation is the tacit recognition that the morphology of form is nothing more, nor less, than a resonance of the structure of human behavior. Through this notion, he directly and incisively confronts the traditional view of structure as embodied meaning or meaning externalized through behavior.

Human behavior is neither a series of
blind reactions to external 'stimuli' nor
the projection of acts which are motivated
by the pure ideas of a disembodied,

112

worldless mind. It is neither exclusively subjective nor exclusively objective but a dialectical interchange between man and the world . . . It is a circular dialectic in which independent beings of the life field, already selected by the structure of the human body, exert a further selective operation on the body's acts. It is out of this dialectical interchange that human meanings emerge.[2]

Similarly, Wolff's music contends that "meanings are neither passively assimilated from an external order . . . as the realists have imagined, nor constructed 'de novo' by a creative mind as the idealists have supposed."[3] Instead, it suggests an identification of the gestures of behavior with the forms issuing therefrom and, ultimately, with the appropriation of meaning.

These attitudes first become apparent in Wolff's pieces from the early '60's such as the *Duo for Violinist and Pianist* (1961) and the string quartet, *Summer* (1961). Clearly, however, even these pieces preserve some vestige of that historical separation of object from action, since certain parameters, in particular, pitch and timbre, are still fixed precompositionally and, thus, maintain a certain degree of control over the composition's unfolding. In contrast, both the composer's ideas and his notation seem to crystallize in such later works as *For 1, 2 or 3 People* (1964) and *Edges* (1968).

For 1, 2 or 3 People is indeterminate with respect to all sonic parameters and any specific morphological propensity. The score consists of ten separate pages, one of which, page III, is reproduced on the following page. One, two or three people may perform, using any instruments, one or more of the score pages in any order. The instructions for performance read, in abridgement, as follows:

113

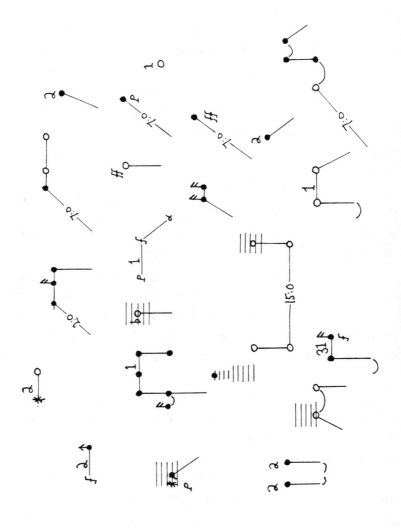

III

Play all that is notated on a page, in any convenient sequence, not repeating anything . . .

Black notes are variously short, up to about one second. With stems as sixteenth notes they are very short. White notes are of any length, sometimes determined by the requirements of coordination . . . A diagonal line towards a note = play that note directly after a preceeding one. A diagonal line away from a note = that note must be followed directly by another.

A vertical line down from a note = play simultaneously with the next sound (both attack and release) . . .

If a line to a note is broken by a number followed, after a colon, by a zero (-2:-) . . . that number of seconds of silence intervene before the required coordination.

⎇ = play after a previous sound has begun, hold until it stops.

O—O = start anytime, hold till another sound starts, finish with it.

⎈ = start at the same time (or as soon as you are aware of it) as the next sound, but stop before it does.

O—O—O = start anytime, hold till another sound starts, continue holding anytime after that sound has stopped.

Horizontal lines joining two notes = a

115

legato from the one to the other . . .

Larger numbers on a line between notes: if black = that number of changes of some aspects(s) of the sound before reaching the next note; in red = that number of changes of the timbre of the first note before reaching the next one.

$\uparrow$ = high in some aspect.[4]

Thus, for instance, the first symbol on the upper left side of page II,

directs the performer to first play any loud sound: then, while holding that sound, to change two aspects of it (volume and timbre for instance); and, finally to move smoothly (legato) to another sound which must be high in some way. In contrast, the symbol near the lower right corner of the page,

directs the performer to play his first sound only after he hears one of the other players produce a sound. He is to hold his sound until the other stops, ending as close as possible to it. In addition, while holding his sound he is instructed to change one aspect of its character (for instance, it might get louder or softer). After this first gesture is completed he is to move directly and smoothly to another pitch which is itself to be followed directly by one more sound produced by himself or any one of the other players.

In listening to this music one is immediately struck by the fact that several renderings of the same notated gesture rarely, if ever, produce patterns which are recognizably similar. "The complexities of this notation are directed less at an arrangement of sounds resulting from the performer's actions than at the conditions under which their actions are to be produced.[5] Thus the notated symbols never determine any particular melodic contour nor any other specific type of sonic configuration. Rather, all that is ever defined symbolically is a complex of interactions between the performers. As the composer himself puts it: "People sometimes ask, why don't you just specify what you want and be done with it? I do! Actions are indicated."[6]

What one hears are the gestures themselves, gestures which are usually taken for granted as the means to an end, but which are here drawn out as an end in themselves. Thus, for example, the idea of playing together takes on importance as an act in itself. Each performance is guided by carefully manipulated behavioral patterns which do not generate products and, as such, do not signify anything beyond their essential characterization as behavior. In this music, one ceases to distinguish between signs and signifiers - forms and the behavior which engenders such forms. This work is not so much a construction in sound, as a situation of action and response defined abstractly through sound. What is perceived as form is the ensemble of these interactions, while the aural result is understood as merely one particular sonic projection of that form. Clearly, that "dialectical interchange" by which form and meaning are engendered is, in this music, embodied within the very substance of its audible structure.

It is significant, also, that in Wolff's music those activities which are represented on the page are usually activities of coordination. In his works actions are intimately tied to responses. First of all, within the framework of *For 1, 2 or 3 People*, it is quite probable that often, while one performer is responding to another, the third may be shaping his next gesture in response to the first. Even more revealing is the fact that, by and large, the actions notated are themselves responses. In this, the composer identifies the notions of action and response as inseparable. Actions are themselves responses which, in turn, generate further responses from others. Acting affects and is, at the same time, itself affected.

> The enigma is that my body simultaneously sees and is seen. That which looks at all things can also look at itself and recognize, in what it sees, the 'other side' of its power of looking. It sees itself seeing; it touches itself touching; it is visible and sensitive for itself. It is not a self through transparence, like thought, which only thinks its object by assimilating it, by constituting it, by transforming it into thought. It is a self through confusion, narcissism, through inherence of the one who sees in that which he sees and through inherence of sensing in the sensed . . . [7]

Robert Ashley's orchestral composition, *in memoriam . . . Crazy Horse* (1964), suggests striking similarities to the Wolff score. Significantly, however, those ideas which both works share in common are dealt with in very different ways and, therefore, are represented graphically through very different systems of notation. Two pages from the score are reprinted here. The instructions read, in part, as follows:

> . . . for 20 or more wind or string or other sustaining instruments in five or more groups of four or more instruments per group.
>
> The instruments of each group should be as closely related as possible.

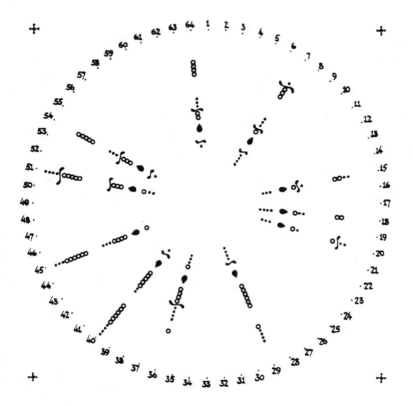

119

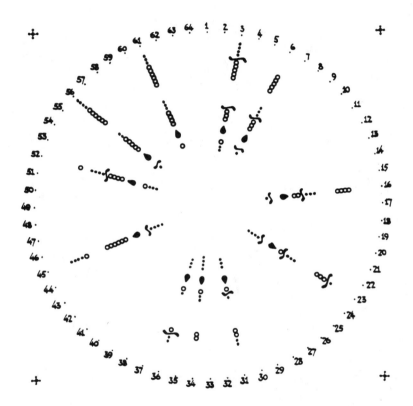

120

Each group plays from one page of the set of 32 pages. Beginning at any radius the players count around the circle allowing one unit of silence for each numbered radius. A sustained sound quality of the appropriate kind is called for upon reaching a radius on which there are number symbols. The inner set of symbols (inside the oval dot) allots a duration to this activity. The outer two sets of symbols specify alternative radii from which to proceed after this duration of activity. Each group decides in advance (in any manner) which direction or schedule of directions it will follow.

The measured units are given for the orchestra as a whole by the conductor and are determined continually and freely by him.

All numbers (durations and radii) are given in sums of the following symbols:

● = 1; ∿ = 5; ○ = 10.

Individual performers determine what is to be played on the basis of their group's obligation to produce a certain density of sound at a certain radius. Plans for assigning various radii or directions of movement to subtle differences in density can be worked out in advance. However, it will be sufficient if the performance involves only the two extremes of ensemble density: as pure (harmonious) as possible; or, as noisy (dissonant) as possible. Any division of the score into semi-circles can be interpreted to represent these two extremes of density.

Individual performers should choose their sounds spontaneously and begin playing at the beginning of a specified duration of activity. Within any duration, then, as soon as all members of the group are playing, individuals may continually adjust (change) their sound activity toward achieving a better realization of the ideal density.

The concept of "density" is intended here to include all aspects of the sound information produced by the ensemble (group), not just density of harmonic spectrum. Thus the term "pure" means...unanimous, similar, redundant, synchronous, integrated, etc., ...in describing the performers' actions (sounds) and implies (1) a lack of individuality among the parts and (2) a high degree of redundancy in successive actions. Conversely, the term "noisy" means...disparate, dissimilar, chaotic, asynchronous, divided, etc., ...in describing the performers' action (sounds) and implies (1) a greater individuality among the parts and (2) a high degree of moment to moment change in successive actions.[8]

For the purpose of clarification, the same two pages of score presented above are again reproduced, annotated in such a way as to facilitate reading and interpretation.

First, it should be noted that the configuration of symbols within the large numbered circle is exactly the same on both score pages. The only difference between these two pages is the placement of this inner configuration with respect to the outer circle. For example, the configuration of symbols found beneath position seven on the numbered circle on the first page is found beneath position twenty-three on the second. In fact, all the configurations on the first page are shifted clockwise sixteen positions on the second.

Symbols within the inner circle determine the duration of each sound activity. These range from three units of time in length to thirteen units of time. The symbols between the inner and outer circles determine the two possible positions along the outer circle to which one may move after performing a given sound event. As nothing concerning this matter is stated in the score it is assumed that one may move clockwise or counterclockwise along the outer circle.

For the purpose of clarification, the following example is offered. If an ensemble within the orchestra is reading the first page, it may begin on any position along the numbered circle. If it does not begin on a position which has symbols beneath it, the ensemble proceeds to move silently in either direction, until it reaches one that does. Let us assume that the ensemble begins on position fifty-nine. It then moves clockwise, following the conductor's beat until it reaches position sixty-four. At this point, the ensemble begins to play and must continue playing for six units of time. When this segment has ended, the group has two options. It may move either to position forty or to position twenty-eight, along the numbered circle. If it chooses forty, it must immediately play for six units of time and then proceed in a manner similar to that just described. If, however, it chooses twenty-eight, which is a silent position, it may then proceed in

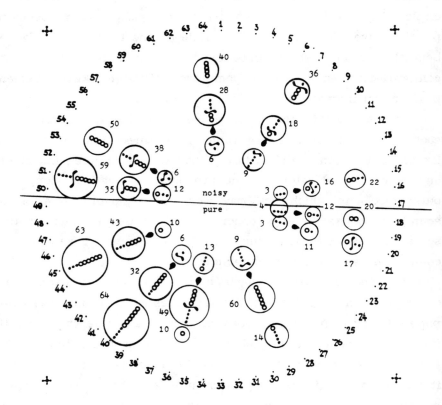

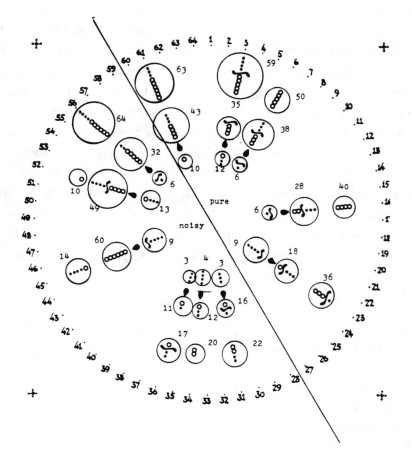

either direction, along the numbered circle, until it reaches a position with symbols on it. All members of each ensemble must follow the same route through the score. The ensembles themselves, however, move independently.

The score has two parts: one, the verbal instructions, determine, in a very general way, the kind of transformations to be used; the other, the graphic symbols, coordinate the activities both within and among the groups. For example, in the annotated score, the circles have been bisected into semi-circles, to one of which is assigned the quality of noisy or dissonant. As such, on the first page, any sound event in the upper half is to be interpreted as noisy and any event in the lower half as pure. Thus, if an ensemble reaches position seven, it performs for nine units of time and during that period strives to make a very noisy sound. If, after this, the ensemble moves to position thirty-six it will play for thirteen units and, during that time, strive to play a very pure sound.

Significantly, the indications of noisy and pure may be interpreted in a variety of ways:

pure (harmonious, simple	vs.	noisy (dissonant, complex)
unisons	vs.	cluster
sine tones	vs.	complex tones
wide registral spacing	vs.	narrow registral spacing
regular rhythmic patterns; one dynamic level	vs.	irregular rhythmic patterns; varying dynamic inflections

Concerning these notions of pure and noisy sound quality it is important to recall the composer's own comments on this subject

126

in the instructions:

> Both of these terms describe antipodal, 'ideal' densities that the ensemble tries to achieve during the course of a particular duration of activity. . . it should be noted that it will defeat the purpose of the performance to play detailed 'realizations' of densities. The preparations for performance should exclude neither the fortuitous initial densities that are the sum of the sound ingredients that the individual players have chosen spontaneously, nor the process involved in the player's attempt to work in an ensemble toward the 'ideal' extreme.[9]

Returning to the annotated score, if an ensemble using the first page reaches position seven, all the members of the ensemble spontaneously and randomly begin playing. As they listen to their sonority each adjusts his own playing in response to what the others are playing, trying to achieve, within the given time limit, as noisy an ensemble sound as possible.

The remainder of the score coordinates activities within and among the ensembles. First of all, the same set of durations (the set within the inner circle: 3 3 4 6 6 9 9 10 12 13) is used on each page of the score and, so, by each ensemble. Each page of the score also determines a different orientation of this duration set to the numbered circle, and each of these, in turn, produces a different distribution of sound events to silences. The result is a random distribution of the various durations for the sound events which still allows coordination among the movements of all the members of any given ensemble.

Any realization of this score must, first of all, be understood as an exploration of the different ways in which these two ideal densities can be achieved by each ensemble of

127

instruments and, ultimately, will be a commentary on the nature of both the types of instruments involved and the characters of those performing as they interact within the constraints of a controlled ensemble situation. For example, an ensemble of violins or oboes can never achieve as pure a sound as an ensemble of flutes or recorders. For one thing, at soft dynamic levels, flute tones are reduced to a sine tone like purity which can never be approached by the other two instruments. Similarly, an ensemble of recorders can never produce as noisy a sound, nor even the same type of noisy sound, as that of an ensemble of trumpets; the recorder being incapable of the violent dynamic contrasts, nor the loud volume levels, available to the trumpet. Clearly, then, the nature of each type of instrument will be a major factor in determining the ways in which the ideal densities are realized and, moreover, will actually determine the limits and character of the imagined 'ideals'.

Another factor which directly affects the unfolding of the piece is the ability of each performer to manipulate his instrument and interact within an ensemble situation. His control over the instrument, and his ability to respond to the others as they together shape their total ensemble sound, will be of singular importance to the shape of each performance and, of course, also, will affect the ensemble's ability to achieve the quality of sound required.

Ashley's composition juxtaposes the different ensembles as they strive independently to achieve their particular densities. Each sound event of the piece begins with a random mass of sound and moves toward one of the two 'ideals'. Each event captures, sonically, the striving of some ensemble to achieve a certain sound. As the initial sonority is sounded, each player begins to adjust his own playing in response to what the others are doing. Of course, as noted above, the ideals may each be realized in many different ways. So, the character of the sound result achieved at the end of each sound event will be determined by the ways in which the members of the ensemble react and interact with one another, as they guide each other and the whole toward some realization of the ideal. Thus, each sound event is not so much a sonic shape as an unfolding interaction. The ideal, itself, is not of interest for its own sonic qualities. Nor, indeed, is the form the sum of a succession of such sonorities. Rather, the ideal is a goal, the repeated and varied strivings for which are, in the end, what are heard as form.

Since the piece is about the striving for some unknown, the notation is purposefully indeterminate. Since it is a true ensemble piece, the activities of each performer must be coordinated and, thus, the graph arises. Because the object is not so much the creation of a specific sound but the striving for a particular sound quality, the composer resorts to a rather suggestive verbal description intimating the qualities toward which the ensemble is to propel itself. What are notated, then are: first, verbally, the goals to be achieved; and then, graphically, the framework within which the various ensembles work to achieve those goals. Sounds themselves are never notated, nor, in fact, are they even the subject of the piece. Rather, once again, what the composer does notate are, verbally, an ideal to be striven for and, graphically, the framework for an ensemble of interactions.

II) Pluralism

A great many of the transformations in musical notation over the past two decades seem to have arisen from the desire to introduce various notions of multiplicity into musical discourse. "Man himself is being forced to reestablish, employ and enjoy his innate 'comprehensivity'."[10] Such a revolutionary conception of form, in turn, necessitates the development of an approach to notation capable of symbolizing a total range of structures rather than any single sonic shape. The evolution of formal schemes

129

which contain the potential for multiple realizations has directed composers to seek new methods of notation enabling them to incorporate their striking visions of multiplicity and comprehensivity.

Neyrac Lux (1978) is a work in five movements for solo guitar by the composer/theorist Pozzi Escot. Both the notation and the structure of its second movement are particularly revealing. The score, reprinted on the following page, consists of two sets of symbols. In the center, there are three collections, each containing seven pitches, all of which are notated on a circular musical stave. On the upper side of the page is a single sequence of numbers arranged in a zig-zag pattern and partitioned in various ways by its alternating vertical and horizontal arrangement of both square and round shaped enclosures.

With respect to the central part of the score - the circular staff - one is instructed to number the three collections in any order. Thus, the seven pitches beamed together on the upper left part of the circle might be labeled collection 2; that on the lower left, 1; and, that on the right, 3. However, it is important to bear in mind that any other labeling is equally acceptable and may be varied from performance to performance.

The number series in the upper right hand corner of the page is to be read, as usual, from upper left to lower right and consists of only the integers 1, 2 and 3. Most striking, is the visual presentation of this series within an alternating sucession of vertical and horizontal boxes and circles which suggest the following partitions:

$$1 \quad 2323 \quad 131 \quad 21 \quad 3232 \quad 121 \quad 3$$

Furthermore, it seems clear that the central pair (2,1) are singled out as of special importance, since these are contained within a circle and all other groupings are contained within

130

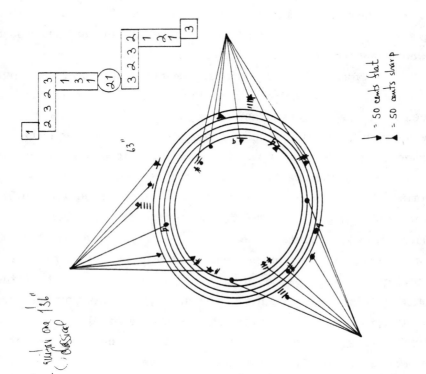

boxes.

Beyond this, only a few very general indications concerning the duration of the movement and silences surrounding it are given. At the top of the score, the indication of one minute and thirty-two seconds is given as the total length of the movement. Below, just to the right of the circular staff is the marking sixty-three seconds which is to be the actual duration of playing time. The remaining thirty-three seconds are silent and are used to separate this movement from its predecessor and successor (twenty-one seconds preceding and twelve following).

In performance, the various elements of the score are put together in such a way that the three pitch groups, now labeled, in some way, as one, two and three are played successively in the order designated by the sequence of numbers. Tempo, the speed at which the tones are played, is determined by the one timing of sixty-three seconds given in the score. This is the total duration of a performance and within only this general constraint the performer sets his tempo. Similarly, no dynamic indications are marked into the score, since the composer believes that these will be determined quite naturally by the speed, order and registral placement of the notes within each group. In general, no instructions are included, because it is the composer's belief that the score visually suggests the structure which it represents, as well as a mode of realization relevant to that structure.

The entire movement is constructed from the additive number series 1, 3, 4, 7, 11, 18 (1 + 3 = 4, 3 + 4 = 7, 4 + 7 = 11, 7 + 11 = 18). From this series the composer determines the following information:

> a) There are 3 pitch collections, each containing 7 pitches.
>
> b) The number sequence contains 18 elements partitioned into 7 groups, two each containing 1, 3, and 4 elements. One

group contains only two elements - the pair in the center. Thus, the visual separation of this group from the others suggests its actual structural isolation from the fundamental series of the piece.

c) The unique nature of this 2-1 pair suggests a further division of the partitioned series into halves:

$$1 \quad 2323 \quad 131 \quad \textcircled{21} \quad 3232 \quad 121 \quad 3$$
$$1 \quad 4 \quad 3 \phantom{\textcircled{21}} \quad 4 \quad 3 \quad 1$$

Each half contains 3 groups, one each of length 1, 3 and 4. Thus, as the notation suggests, the central pair serves a pivotal role in the composition's organization.

Central to any exploration of the notation employed here is the fact that the three pitch collections can be ordered in any way desired. As such, the movement is left open to multiple interpretations and, from one performance to the next, its form will be encountered in a variety of different sonic garb. The work's notation suggests this separation between form and materials quite dramatically, since the three pitch collections are presented apart from the number series by which they are shaped. Moreover, the multiplicity which such a separation implies is also captured graphically in the circularity of the musical staff, itself an unambiguous image of plurality. Thus, in several ways, the notation of this piece depicts, quite vividly, an image of structure created so as to admit any number of equilavent sonic representations. It is a striking vision of abstraction and of that sense of universality which such abstraction engenders.

Significant parallels are suggested to several works of the visual artist Sol LeWitt. In his drawing for *Wall Markings* (1968),

LeWitt outlines what is essentially a score which, with the exception of certain details, suggests amazing similarities to the second movement of the Escot guitar piece. *Wall Markings* consists of two systems, as the artist refers to them, and two very different modes of realization. Each system is to be articulated visually by both of these sets of graphic materials. LeWitt's drawing, then, contains within its framework two very different visual realizations for each structure which it proposes. As such, the work seems to demonstrate a certain independence of form from its materials and points to many of those same notions of abstraction and multiplicity which were encountered in the notation and music of Pozzi Escot's *Neyrac Lux*.

Reflecting many of these same concerns, as also revealed through its notation, is *Variations II* (1961) of John Cage. The score for this piece consists of eleven separate transparent sheets, six having straight lines and five having points.

The sheets are to be superimposed partially or wholly separated on an suitable surface. Drop perpendiculars by means of any rule obtaining readings thereby for 1) frequency, 2) amplitude, 3) timbre, 4) duration, 5) point of occurrence in an established period of time, 6) structure of event (number of sounds making up an aggregate or constellation). A single use of all sheets yields thirty determinations. When, due to 6), more are necessary, change the position of the sheets with respect to one another before making them. Any number of readings may be used to provide a program of any length. [11]

Any realization of this score is the result of a particular configuration fashioned from some superimposition of these sheets.

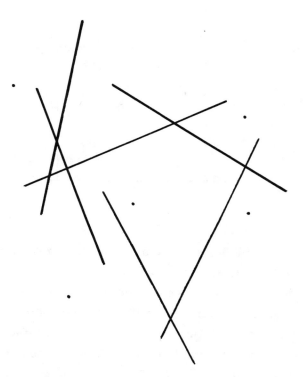

The sonic structure resulting from such a superimposition will invariably be that of some statistical correlation of several distributions of sound elements.

For the sake of clarity, examples will be drawn from a simpler score, consisting of fewer components than the original. In this situation, constructed by the author, a score with only three lines and four dots will be used. By superimposing these elements the following configuration might arise:

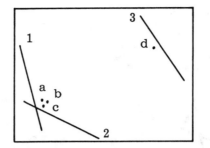

Here, the dots and lines have been labeled, respectively: a, b, c, and d; and, 1, 2, 3.

The dots represent sonic events and the lines are given assignments as sonic parameters. Let us say, for instance, that 1 = duration, 2 = pitch and 3 = volume. If a dot falls close to 1, it represents a short sound; close to 2, a low sound; and, close to 3, a soft sound; far away from 1, a long sound; far away from 2, a high sound; and, far away from 3, a loud sound. Since there is no point of occurrence parameter in this example, it will be assumed that the performer or performers may read through the dots in any order. With respect to this particular configuration, then, it seems clear that there will be three times as many short sounds as long and three times as many low sounds as high, since three dots fall close to 1 and 2 and one far away. Also, there will be three times as many loud sounds as high, since three dots fall close to 1 and 2 and one far away. Also, there will be three times as many loud sounds as there are soft, since only one dot is close to 3 while three are far away. This information is summarized in the following chart:

136

	close	far
1	3	1
2	3	1
3	1	3

The structure of this composition, then, consists of three distributions of dots, one distribution over each line.

It is important to note however, that there are actually two aspects of this structure (this configuration) which have been revealed through the chart. First, the total available range of each parameter has been partitioned into only two general areas: close (soft, short, low) and far (loud, long, high). Second, a density ratio of 3:1 has been determined. As such, over the course of any reading of this particular realization, one of the two partitioned areas of any parameter will have three times as many sounds as the other.

Next, it should be observed that the configuration also determined a specific correlation among those distributions. Roughly speaking, the majority of sounds will be short, low and loud while only one-third as many will be long, high and soft. More precisely, the 3:1 density ratio is assigned to the two partitions of each parameter in the following manner:

duration	:	(short / long)
		3 : 1
pitch	:	(low : high)
		3 : 1
volume	:	(loud : soft)
		3 : 1

137

This particular assignment of the 3:1 ratio to the three parameters tends to group, on the one hand all short/low/loud sounds together and, on the other hand, all the long/high/soft ones. These groupings follow naturally from the respective densities of occurrence within the partitions of the various parameters. In other words, there are three times as many short/low/loud sounds as there are long/high/soft ones:

short/low/loud : long/high/soft
3 : 1

Thus, the specific assignments of the density ratio to the three sets of partitions results in a correlation among the elements of those partitions.

To summarize: first, the total available range of each parameter is partitioned into two broadly defined regions (low-high, loud-soft, short-long), as a result of the configuration of dots over each line; second, an association is made between members of these pairs (short/low/loud, long/high/soft), as a result of the configuration of the lines; and third, a density ratio is determined (the result of which will be the sounding of three times as many sounds of the short/low/loud type as there will be of the long/high/soft type). The final aural result is, then, that of a statistical distribution of sounds over several parameters and one specific correlation of those distributions. If several performers were to read through the configuration several times, there would sound approximately three times as many short/low/loud sounds than long/high/soft ones. The order of performance of the dots is irrelevant and will in no way alter this outcome, since the overall statistical results will remain unchanged despite the particular order in which the sounds are heard.

It is, however, important to recognize that the score does not fix any one such configuration. Rather, the composer presents as his score the materials by which any such configuration may be fashioned. As such, the score contains within it the full range of all possible configurations of six lines and five dots and, consequently, the full range of statistical structures to which these configurations give rise. Thus, it cannot really be said that any one specific statistical structure is the structure of *Variations II*. Rather, the structure of this composition is the complete range of all such statistical complexes made available by the composer through the score. Indeed, with respect to this notion it would seem significant that Cage allows the use of many different realizations of the score within any single performance (see instructions: "Any number of readings may be used to provide a program of any length."[12]) Clearly, then, each performance may contain many suggestions of the work's inherent multiplicity, since it may freely sample from the range of structures which the composition's superstructure engenders.

Cage has integrated into the structure of his piece the very processes by which that structure evolves. Moreover, the realization of these processes is left open, to be completed by those assembling a performance. *Variations II*, then, is one, large, comprehensive system which itself represents the total accumulation of its many constituent realizations. As such, the score represents a structure *in potentia* since it symbolizes, graphically, not just one specific statistical distribution but, rather, the mechanism for constructing an entire range of such distributions.

"A composer who hears sounds will try to find a notation for sounds. One that has ideas will find one that expresses his ideas, leaving their interpretation free, in confidence that his ideas have been accurately and concisely notated."[13] Though many composers who have striking and revealing insights still do employ traditional notation, it seems clear that, with respect to the music of the past two decades, an era has emerged wherein

139

the notation of method often takes prominence over the notation of sound. This has led to a flourishing of creative energy devoted almost exclusively to the discovery of unconventional methods for notating musical compositions. As a result, recent compositional activity has witnessed a shift in emphasis away from the creation of sonic structures, toward the creation of more precise ways of notating activities and attitudes. This change, in turn, has brought to light a multitude of hitherto unexplored facets of our perception, creation and understanding of musical structure.

1) Cornelius Cardew, *Treatise Handbook* (London: C. F. Peters, 1971), p. xv.

2) Maurice Merleau-Ponty, *The Structure of Behavior* (Boston: Beacon Press, 1967), p. xiv.

3) *Ibid.*, p. xv.

4) Christian Wolff, *For 1, 2 or 3 People* (New York: C. F. Peters, 1964), p.1.

5) David Behrman, "What Indeterminate Notation Determines," *Perspectives on Notation and Performance*, Benjamin Boretz and Edward Cone eds. (New York: W. W. Norton Co., 1976), p. 89.

6) Christian Wolff, record liner notes, *John Cage and Christian Wolff* (Mainstream Records, MS 5015), p. 2.

7) Maurice Merleau-Ponty, *The Primacy of Perception* (Evanston, Illinois: Northeastern University Press, 1964), pp. 162 - 163.

8) Robert Ashley, *in memoriam...Crazy Horse, Source Magazine* (Davis California: Composer/Performer Editions, 1967), p. 42.

9) *Ibid.*, p. 42.

10) R. Buckminster Fuller, *Operating Manual for Spaceship Earth* (New York: Simon and Schuster, 1969), p. 44.

11) John Cage, *Variations II* (New York: C. F. Peters, Corporation, 1961), p. 1.

12) *Ibid.*, p. 1.

13) Cardew, *op. cit.*, p. iii.

The Tools of My Trade

Alvin Lucier

In the summer of 1960 I arrived in Venice. I had just received a Fulbright Scholarship to Rome and had come over to Italy early to attend the summer sessions of the Benedetto Marcello Conservatory. Since boyhood I had longed to live in Europe. My musical education had been solidly based on French, German, and Italian music (at Yale, Charles Ives had hardly been mentioned and John Cage was considered a clown), so it was only natural to regard this part of the world as my spiritual home. I rented a studio on the Grand Canal, along with an upright piano which was delivered by gondola, and was ready to continue composing music in the neo-classical style I had learned to admire at Yale and Brandeis.

My first project in Europe was to be a sonata for small trumpet and harpsichord, commissioned by Armando Ghitalla, then Associate First Trumpet of the Boston Symphony Orchestra. My intention was to write a set of variations on a theme of Monteverdi. For some time I had been attracted to the charming echo-duets between pairs of oboes and violins which appear in the *Deposuit* of the *Magnificat* of the *Vespers of 1610*, and I planned to base my sonata on this material. Perhaps it was that the disparity between the blown and plucked sounds of the trumpet and harpsichord (Monteverdi had used pairs of similar instruments to create his echoes) made the illusion of echoes impossible or I was simply struck by the predictable identity

143

crisis of the American expatriate in Europe, but my enthusiasm for the project sputtered and I soon stopped working.

Around that time the Studio Fonologia at the Italian Radio in Milan, which had been so active under Berio, was still accessible to composers and I got permission through the Fulbright office in Rome to work there for two winter weeks in 1961. The accepted working procedure in that studio was to record on tape a vocabulary of sounds, which you would then cut into five- or six-foot lengths, label, and paste up on the walls around the studio. As you needed sounds for your compositions, you would cut off various lengths of desired material - so many centimeters for so much time, depending on the speed of your tape recorder - splice them together and mix them into a final product. I will never forget the excitement of working directly with sounds on tape for the first time - the physicality of that activity! - but no amount of splicing or mixing could change my old compositional habits and I failed to come up with even a short piece that I felt was worthy of this exciting new medium.

It wasn't until several years later, in 1965, that I felt I had produced a satisfactory work with electronic means. I was teaching and directing choral music at Brandeis at that time and happened to meet physicist Edmond Dewan, who was then doing brain wave research for the Air Force. He generously lent me his apparatus, consisting of a pair of electrodes, a differential amplifier, and a band pass filter, set to a band-width just wide enough to let the 10 Hz alpha waves flow through and at the same time reject unwanted electrical and ambient noise. I began experimenting with Dewan's equipment for long hours in the Brandeis Electronic Music Studio, which was then located in the basement of the university library. At first I could only generate short bursts of alpha, but after some practice found that I could sustain trains of almost indefinite lengths. I was struck by the piston-like excursions of the loudspeaker cones as they were driven by the sub-sonic bursts and decided to use this power to excite a battery of percussion instruments, including cymbals, gongs, tympani, bass and snare drums, by directly coupling them to loudspeakers, deployed in various locations throughout the space. I ignored the advice of my Brandeis colleagues - to record brain waves and then process them as mere sound material, using conventional studio techniques (splicing would have seemed like brain surgery to me) - and was content to allow the natural flow of brain waves in live performance to provide the structure of the performance.

Besides being the first musical work in history to use brain waves, *Music for Solo Performer* was also, more importantly, the first in which a performer is asked to produce sound by keeping absolutely still. (Alpha is blocked while the brain is occupied with activities such as physical movement and visualization and can be set free by attaining a state of quiet non-visualization.) Performing music while in a state of meditation, an activity forced on me by the nature of the material, was a memorable experience for me. It completely changed my conception of composition and performance and led to the attentive rather than manipulative attitude towards materials which typified most of my subsequent works.

Following *Solo Performer*, I began a series of pieces which explored the acoustic characteristics of natural and architectural spaces. *Chambers*, the first of these, composed in 1968, treats found objects, such as conch shells, teapots, and briefcases, as portable environments or miniature rooms which may be made to sound in various ways, often by the insertion of battery-operated radios, cassette recorders, and toys. As performers carry these resonant objects through indoor and outdoor spaces, the listener compares the acoustic characteristics of both large and small environments as they impinge their personalities on one another.

The second piece in this series, *Vespers* (1969), is based on the sound-sending and sound-receiving acuity of bats and other nocturnal experts in the art of echolocation. Any number of players, armed with Sondols (*sonar-dolphin*), specially-designed hand-held pulse generators, which emit fast, short clicks whose repetition rate can be varied, move through darkened rooms, discovering routes to goals and avoiding obstacles by listening to echoes from reflective surfaces in the environment. As they do so, they provide listeners with an acoustic signature of that environment. It wasn't until several years later that it struck me that this work was the finished version of the little trumpet sonata I had begun and abandoned in Venice years before. The title should have told me sooner. Now, however, the echoes are real, not symbolic. They exist in physical space; they don't have to stand for anything else.

In *"I am sitting in a room"* (1970) several sentences of recorded speech are simultaneously played back in a room and re-recorded there many times. As the repetitive process continues, those frequencies common to the original spoken statement and the resonant frequencies of the room are gradually eliminated. The space acts as a filter; the speech is transformed into pure sound.

The last work in this series, *Quasimodo the Great Lover* (1972), employs several microphone-amplifier-loudspeaker systems to relay sound materials over long distances, through indoor and outdoor spaces, earth, water, metal, ice and other materials, until they reach a state of unrecognizability. During the process they capture and carry the acoustic characteristics of the spaces through which they travel. Although *Room* and *Quasimodo* were written at different times and are based on very different ideas - one, the articulation of room resonances, the other, the transformation of sound by means of long distance transmission - both use repetitive processes to produce a desired result. A difference is that *Room* is made up of closed loops, material which comes back upon itself, while *Quasimodo* consists of chained segments, each of which is conceived as moving in one forward direction.

In 1973 I began working on a number of works which explore the spatial characteristics of sound itself. *Still and Moving Lines of Silence in Families of Hyperbolas*, a large-scale work for players, singers, dancers and unattended percussion, completed in 1974, is based on standing waves and related phenomena. Simply put, if a pure wave from a sine tone oscillator emanates from two loudspeakers or one loudspeaker and a reflective wall, crests and troughs of loud and soft sound will form in hyperbolic curves, spreading out on either side of an imaginary line midway between the loudspeakers. The lower the frequency, the fewer and wider apart the curves are; the higher the frequency, the more and closer together, Furthermore, if the two waves, tuned slightly apart, are sounded, each from a separate loudspeaker, the beat patterns that result will cause the crests and troughs to spin in elliptical patterns through space, in the direction of the lower sounding loudspeaker. In a complete performance of this work, any number of dancers seek out and move in troughs of quiet sound; singers create vibratos of different speeds by singing against sustained sounds; instrumental players spin hyperbolas to and from themselves and loudspeakers positioned around them; and snare drums are made to vibrate sympathetically in continually-changing rhythmic patterns, as crests of loud sound travel across their heads.

Hyperbolas was followed by *Bird and Person Dyning* (1975), which employs a binaural microphone system to locate and position phantom sonic images in space. A toy electronic bird, which emits a call consisting of a downward sweep followed by a series of chirps, is placed in the middle of a performance

147

space. A single performer wears a pair of miniature microphones in his or her ears, routed through limiters and amplifiers to a pair of stereo loudspeakers, played at high enough volume levels to produce feedback. From time to time combination tones between the sounds of the chirping bird and strands of feedback are produced, according to the principles of acoustical heterodyning. If the feedback happens to sound below the pitches of the chirping bird, the phantoms are heard tracking the original chirps in parallel motion, at pitch intervals determined by the intervals between the two original sounds. If the feedback happens above the bird sounds, the images will be mirrors of the original, sweeping upward from low to high. Occasionally double or even triple strands of feedback will occur, creating multiple images in parallel and contrary motion simultaneously. Because of the locative properties of the binaural system, the phantoms often seem to place themselves in various parts of the space.

Outlines of Persons and Things (1976) explores the diffractive properties of sound. Clusters of high frequency pure waves, emanating from loudspeakers, illuminate objects opaque to sound, casting shadows around them. In order to perceive the shadow vividly, one of the three components in the system - sound source, person or thing around which sounds flow, or listener (human being or microphone) - must move, so that comparisons in time may be made. And since it is awkward to move loudspeakers or people during a performance of such sonic delicacy, a dancer is asked to move in front of a stack of loudspeakers and a performer to scan a fixed object with a directional microphone. The listener hears both the direct and diffracted sound and compares something moving to something fixed.

Most of these works have had to do with making the

inaudible audible. Pieces such as *Solo Performer*, *Vespers*, *"I am sitting in a room"*, and *Hyperbolas* uncover sounds or aspects of sound which we seldom hear because of our concern with musical language. In 1972 I took this idea in a slightly different direction with a series of works which have to do with "seeing" sound. In the *Queen of the South*, sounds produced by electronic or acoustic means are fed, via audio transducers, to the undersides of plates of metal, wood, glass and other similar materials upon which is strewn sand, salt, coffee, tea and other fine-grained stuffs. As the sounds excite the plates the strewn material scatters, forming visual patterns, determined by the structure of the plates and the volumes, frequencies, timbres and envelopes of the sounds. Any number of closed circuit video cameras view the changing imagery and display it on video monitors. Several years later, in 1977, I made a work called *Tyndall Orchestrations* which explores the relationship between sound and flame. By inserting the tips of Bunsen burners into vertically-clamped glass tubes, it is possible to make the tubes sing by exciting the resonant frequencies of the tubes by action of the flame. Small changes in gas pressure cause slight shifts in pitch and, if conditions are right, sounds from one tube may reinforce resonances in other tubes, by sympathetic vibration. A naked flame, on the other hand, may be made to jump and momentarily assume various shapes in response to certain high-pitched sounds.

Music on a Long Thin Wire, also from 1977, began as a physics demonstration in a musical acoustics class I was teaching at Wesleyan with physicist John Trefny. We had stretched four feet of metal wire across a table top, the ends of which were connected to the outputs of an oscillator-driven amplifier. A horseshoe magnet straddled the wire at one end, causing the wire to vibrate due to the interaction of its flux field and the current flowing through the wire. I began having an artist's vision of what a very long wire - say, 200 miles long - would sound like and decided to transform the experiment into a musical piece. Compared to a short wire, I knew that a very long one would sound amazing, that a quantitative scale-change would cause a qualitative sound-change, and that the wire would take on a life of its own. For practical purposes I had to be content with extending the wire down the length of whatever space is available. To date, the longest has been 80 feet through the oval of the rotunda of the old U.S. Custom House in New York City. For installation of any time length I tune the driving oscillator, which puts a steady state current of a certain frequency into the wire, only once; then let changes caused by fatigue, heating, cooling, air currents, expansion and contraction, and other physical changes in the system or the environment determine the pitch, harmonic, timbral, rhythmic and other musical parameters.

In 1978 I made two pieces having to do with the visualization of sound. *Ghosts* is a simple piece in which one performer, carrying a sound-sensitive light, searches through a pure sound wave environment for bumps of sound, caused by imperfections (reflections, absorptions, etc.) in the environment, which cause the light to turn on. Over time, it draws with the light the three-dimensional shapes of these imperfections. *Directions of Sounds from the Bridge* explores the directionality of sound flow from stringed instruments. The bridge of an upright-standing cello or other stringed instrument is driven by the sound of a pure wave oscillator. Several sound sensitive lights, similar to the one used in *Ghosts*, are positioned equidistantly around the instrument. As the waves sweep up through the range of the instrument the sounds flow out of it in different directions at different volumes and the lights are activated, showing, however crudely, the sound shapes that form around it.

150

A companion piece to the above work is *Shapes of the Sounds from the Board* (1979-80), for piano. As a pianist plays single long tones in a rising chromatic scale, allowing each one to decay to silence, microphones listen to the spatial movement of the sounds, caused by phase differences along the piano strings. This information is amplified for listeners. Each note has its own unique moving shape which may be heard by the careful listener. Sound-sensitive floor lamps, placed around the piano, turn on and off, blink, dim and fade away in response to the attack, sustain and decay characteristics of the piano sounds.

Music for Pure Waves, Bass Drums and Acoustic Pendulums (1980) continues this line of investigation. Loudspeakers, from which emanate a slowly-rising pure tone, are positioned directly behind four bass drums. A ping-pong ball is suspended in front of each drum. As the pure sounds flow through the drumheads, causing them to vibrate, the balls bounce against the heads in ever-changing rhythmic patterns, determined by the pitches and volumes of the waves and the resonant characteristics of the drums. As the waves pass through the drums' resonant regions, the heads vibrate more violently, causing the balls to bounce further away, sometimes up to a length of two feet. If, at the moment a ball returns to a drumhead, the head itself is on an outward phase of its vibratory cycle, the ball is again bounced outward and the size of the pendular swing is maintained or even increased. If, however, the ball meets the head on an inward or negative phase, its motion is dampened and the ball may be stopped dead.

Through the years I have composed a handful of other works which do not exactly fit the categories of the above-mentioned pieces. Two early works written in Rome in 1962 explore the possibilities of graphic notation. In *Action Music for Piano*, only the physical gestures of the pianist (it was written for Fredric Rzewski) are notated, the sounds occur as residue.

The piece is concerned more with the act of playing the piano than the musical results of such playing and most of the performer's activities occur in the space around the instrument. Perhaps the distancing of performer from instrument was a response to being far from home. In any case it formed the basis of later works concerned with identity (*Duke of York*), geographical location (*Bird and Person Dyning*), performance by remote control (*Directions of Sounds from the Bridge*) and sounds sent over long distances (*Quasimodo the Great Lover*). The second of these early works, *Song for Soprano*, a setting of Yeats' pessimistic poem, "That the Night Come," used a cut-out technique to match words and sounds in a semi-random way.

There have been three works that involve the modification of the human voice by electronic means: *North American Time Capsule* (1967) utilizes a vocoder to scramble an overabundance of diverse vocal and instrumental material; *The Only Talking Machine of Its Kind in the World* (1969), in which a tape delay system in the form of a mandala cures a stammerer's speech; and in *The Duke of York* (1972) one or more electronic music synthesizers alter a series of human utterances, finally creating a new vocal personality.

There have been two works which employ digital technology: *RMSIM 1* (1972) uses a computer to simulate changes in the materials and dimensions of a source room, creating a chain of imaginary rooms; and in *Clocker* (1978), a biologically-controlled digital delay system slows down and speeds up the ticks of a real clock.

There has been only one work so far which explores solar energy for musical purposes. *Solar Sounder 1*, a totally sun-powered sound sculpture, made in collaboration with electronic designer John Fullemann, is permanently installed in the foyer of the City Savings Bank in Middletown, Connecticut. As sunlight falls on three photovoltaic panels at different angles and intensities, at different times of day and year and in various weather conditions, the speed, rhythm, pitch and timbre of electronically-generated pulsed sounds change accordingly.

A spate of recent commissions has generated a miscellany of works in various media: *Job's Coffin* (1979), in which carefully tuned sound waves cause to open the drawers of a small chest of drawers (for oboist Joseph Celli); *Shy Words* (1980) for voices, tape delay system and moving loudspeakers (for the Chicago Symphony of Composers); and a *Lullaby* for my daughter Amanda, in which wind-like sounds are gently blown around a child's head in ways that suggest the motions and shapes of real and imaginary phenomena (for a collection of lullabies edited by pianist Doris Hays).

At the time of this writing, my most recent completed work, and one which I have thought about for some time, is *Reflections of Sounds from the Wall*. It was realized for the first time in March, 1981, in the almost echo-free soundstage of Media Study/Buffalo. A fairly high frequency (2600 Hz) square wave, chosen for its short wavelength and odd-harmonic content, is beamed at a moving 4 x 8 ft. plywood baffle, which reflects the waves around the room, creating vivid stereo images, accompanied by subtle shifts in harmonic structure. *Reflections*, I suppose, relates directly to *Vespers*, in which moving sounds are reflected off fixed walls; in this work, on the contrary, sound waves from a fixed source reflect off moving surfaces.

There are some unfinished works, including *Whistlers*, begun in 1967, involving the reception of magnetic disturbances from the ionosphere; and an unperformed piece, *Gentle Fire*, in which recorded sounds are transformed into other sounds by electronic means; and a recent piece, *Self-Portrait*, for blown sounds and wind anemometer. As the blades of the anemometer spin at speeds determined by the flow of air from the sound source - a human mouth or the edge of a flute embouchure - objects in the environment as well as the performer himself are

153

alternately illuminated and concealed by light and shadows produced by the spinning blades. There are also several other miscellaneous pieces, mostly student efforts and early theater works, and there may even be one or two I have forgotten.

Of the thirty or so works mentioned above the great majority are based on some form of electronic technology. Several, including *Room*, *Quasimodo*, *Bird and Person*, and *Shapes*, used basic or specialized high fidelity studio equipment: microphones, tape recorders, amplifiers, loudspeakers. Many more - *Solo Performer*, *Vespers*, *Hyperbolas*, *Directions*, *Reflections* among them - employ industrial or scientific test equipment, including differential amplifiers, pulse, sine and square wave oscillators, audio transducers and the like. Acoustical test equipment is, by its very nature, free of content. What goes into a material or environment to be tested must be neutral so that the results are unbiased. And as the process of testing, probing, or exploring often forms the basis of compositional structure and performance activity in my work, these devices are perfect tools for me to use. Only one - *The Duke of York* - specifically calls for a commercially-available electronic music synthesizer. Synthesizers are general purpose musical instruments usually designed to be played with keyboards. The complex routing, patching or matrix procedures suggested by the physical construction of such instruments, imply a musical language of some sort, which renders them useless for my purposes. Often, however, I find it useful to isolate and utilize one or two modules of a particular synthesizer. *Solar Sounder 1*, for example, consists of one Aries pulse wave oscillator and a resonant filter. But since the idea in *The Duke of York* was to create a synthetic vocal identity by an additive layering process, I felt that the synthesizer was the appropriate tool for this purpose.

Three of the pieces - *Solo Performer*, *Shapes*, *Quasimodo* -

154

take amplification seriously. The first of these raises "sounds" to a level of audibility; the second enhances a faint audible phenomenon; the third simply extends the ranging distance of sound. None relies on amplification to make sound loud for aesthetic reasons. And in those works which use sound to drive physical systems - wires, stringed instruments, bass drums, for example - volume levels at the input stage are selected to drive those systems efficiently and without distortion.

Six of the compositions use sine wave oscillators as the basic sound source. In three of these - *Hyperbolas*, *Outlines*, and *Ghosts* - the pure waves are valued for their spatial characteristics; because of their purity (all fundamental, no harmonics) they enable the listener to perceive the geographical placement of sound in space. In the other three - *Wire*, *Bridge*, *Pendulums* - a pure sound source is necessary so that what happens in and to those media is clearly perceptible. Any material with personality would only blur the phenomena.

In most of the pieces there is little or no musical language at the input stage. This is so that the phenomena may be explored in as unbiased a way as possible. There is virtually none in *Wire*, *Outlines*, or *Ghosts*, only strands of pure tones which create steady state environments in which the fluctuations inherent in the systems can be clearly perceived. I think of them as canti firmi, out of which the music flows. In *Directions* and *Pendulums* there are only rising sound sweeps of pure tones, and even those move so slowly that no pitch change is noticeable. The sweeps cause pure waves at all frequencies within the sweeps to test all possible resonances of the cello and bass drums respectively. The microscopic slowness of the sweeps is necessary so that no resonance, spatial movement or rhythmic pattern is missed by moving too fast. Actually the speed of the sweeps is merely proportional to the very small size of the intervals at which resonsnt regions may be distinguished

155

Shapes of the Sounds from the Board also employs an upward sweep, except that the chromatic scale structure of the piano keyboard renders a coarser resolution of the spatial mapping of sound flow from the instrument. The intervals between the notes are just too large.

In the same way continuity, that is, what follows what, is not based on temporal, textural, timbral, or other kinds of contrast. It often consists simply in letting the sound material flow according to its own laws. In any performance of *Music for Solo Performer*, for example, there is always enough variation in alpha: it fluctuates in frequency (and rhythm), and displays a wide range of amplitude, from very quiet pulses to sharp over-driving bursts of sound. I am often amused when someone suggests that a 10 Hz square wave would serve as well in performing this work. And in *Vespers* the changes in speed of the pulses are determined by the echoes that are produced, not by a desire to create interesting rhythmic patterns. Textural structures are inadvertently made as players stop to empty out the acoustic space, then recommence echolocating. And in *Reflections* the slight timbral changes one hears are a by-product of phase-shifting, as the sound waves reflect off the baffle at various angles. In most of my work, whatever changes do occur are almost never determined by conscious mental (compositional) or physical (performance) activity but rather by something inherent in or even external to a given system: variations in the resonant characteristics of different drums, as in *Pendulums*, or by a force of nature, for example, the presence or absence of sunlight in *Solar Sounder 1*.

The larger formal structures are often uni-directional, linear and focused. The form of *"I am sitting in a room,"* for example, is a simple repetitive process of recycling pre-recorded speech into a room many times. And while the process does not change, the rate of speed of the modification of the speech does. It has its own shape, irrespective of and superimposed upon the

156

regularity of the recording process. This shape changes, of course, from version to version, as different room are explored. There is also a third variable in this work and that is the point at which the intelligible speech becomes unintelligible. It is a sort of lever with a sliding fulcrum which is re-positioned by each listener and may vary from performance to performance, even of the same recorded version.

In those works in which performers move throughout the space, the designs they trace as they do so closely resemble the simple forms described above. In *Outlines* a dancer moves in a perpendicular line away from the front of the loudspeakers, causing his or her sound shadow to grow smaller and sharper, the farther away she gets; and in *Bird and Person Dyning* the performer walks directly toward the electronic bird, making small angles and curves to find good places for heterodyning. Even in *Reflections* the motorized baffle crawls across the floor in slow zig-zag patterns in order to reflect sound waves to various parts of the room. The dancers in *Hyperbolas,* of course, follow the quiet valleys of sound whose shapes are described in the title of the work. It is no coincidence, either, that the verbal and visual analogs of the wave forms used in many works are simple geometric shapes: sine curves (*Hyperbolas, Wire, Directions, Ghosts, Pendulums*), square waves (*Reflections*), pulse waves (*Vespers, Solar Sounder 1*).

The ideas for these pieces come from a variety of sources, including books and articles on musical and architectural acoustics, occasional conversations with scientists, and observations of natural phenomena. Sometimes the idea comes directly from the book or article, for example Hans Jenny's *Cymatics* (*The Queen of the South*); Tyndall's *On Sound* (*Tyndall Orchestrations*); or a recent article in Scientific American on piano sound (*Shapes of the Sound from the Board*). By the same token, Edmond Dewan not only gave me the idea for

Music for Solo Performer but later described to me the recycling procedure I used in *"I am sitting in a room,"* as he heard it explained by loudspeaker designer Amar Gopel Bose. At other times the readings either clarify technical problems I happen to be working on at the time - Donald R. Griffin's books on echolocation, *Listening to the Dark* and *Echoes of Bats and Men*, gave me the information I needed to complete *Vespers* - or provide knowledge of a more general nature which I may later use in a transformed state. For example, Winston E. Kock's writings on sound waves and light waves got me interested in the diffraction of sound.

Occasionally, a piece of equipment will inspire a particular work. *Vespers* could not have been made without the existence of Sondols, manufactured by Listening, Incorporated in Arlington, Massachusetts for boat owners and the blind; *The Duke of York* was a parody of synthesizer technology; a delicately-engineered wind anemometer (its blades spin on diamonds) is currently inspiring *Self-Portrait;* an audio digital delay system designed by composer Paul De Marinis gave me the idea for *Clocker,* in which time is apparently sped up and slowed down.

A few of the works take as their points of departure nineteenth century scientific experiments. In addition to *The Queen of the South,* based on E. P. Chladni's (1756-1827) demonstrations of sound vibrating in various media, and *Tyndall Orchestrations,* a recasting of John Tyndall's (1820-1893) work on the relationship between sound and flame, *Pendulums* is a musical realization of the old bell and pithball experiment found in a more modern textbook on sound by British physicists Catchpool and Slatterly. The oldest historical reference in my work, except of course to the use of echolocation, a technique perfected by bats millions of years ago, is to the Pythagorean monochord which was the model for *Music on a Long Thin Wire.*

Often the excecution of a work closely resembles the natural

158

situation or scientific experiment upon which it is based. In *Solo Performer*, for example, the performer produces alpha in much the same way one would produce it during and EEG examination. The poetry and drama of the situation are maintained; only the environment and output are changed, from hospital to concert hall and from visual readout to sound. In *Vespers* the Sondol players simulate nocturnal activities of bats; they move through dark spaces guided by reflected sound, as in sonar. The physical set-up of *Music on a Long Thin Wire* is exactly the same as that of the laboratory demonstration upon which it is based, except for the enormous scale which helps give the work its visual and sonic personality.

There is not, on the surface at least, a social or political message in any of my works. For the same reason that language or structure interferes with the clarity of the perception of the phenomenon to be explored, any idea foreign to the musical one, that directs the mind away from the sounding process, would only be distracting and out of place. But the fact that many of my works employ very simple means to achieve their ends, even though those ends may be complex, reveals a not-too-hidden message about the use of energy in a world of diminishing resources.

Nowhere is this idea as well expressed as in *Solar Sounder 1*. Even though John Fullemann designed this system to operate on very little power, it was still necessary to choose sound material which would use as little as possible. Fullemann explained that short sounds with plenty of silences between them require fewer watts than long sustained ones. He therefore suggested we use pulse waves - short, sharp electronic sounds which need be "on" only a fraction of a complete duty cycle to be audible. Not only do they use very little energy, but variations in their pulse width, that is, the length of time they are on or off, create lovely asymmetrical rhythmic cells as well as sounds of varying tone color. (One of the characteristics of the pulse wave is that its overtone structure is determined by its pulse width.)

Observing the world of nature is for me, as it has been for countless composers and artists for centuries, often a source for a piece. Echoes from mountains, ripples on a pond, waves hitting a beach, even puffs of wind have given me material for such works as *Vespers*, *Hyberbolas*, *Self-Portrait*, the *Lullaby* for my daughter, and other works having to do with the movement of sounds. Mine was a New Hampshire childhood of creek-floats, canoe trips (pungent experiences of wave motion), mountain hikes and woodland walks. Coupled with early readings of Robert Frost's poems, in which natural phenomena stand for states of mind, these experiences drew me toward the exploration of these phenomena for musical purposes. (Frost also believed that the penetration of matter by science was the single most important activity in his part of the twentieth century.) Later, readings of Hemingway's works led me to the minimalism my pieces exhibit time and time again. Hemingway felt that if you knew your subject well enough, what you chose to leave out would still be present in the work. I have often thought that the unnecessary complexity in much new music serves to compensate for the lack of clear ideas; you add apparent richness to hide poverty. Often as I start making a work I imagine the need for more material than is necessary - two or more driving oscillators in *Wire*, for example, or four baffles moving in different directions in *Refelctions*. But as soon as I understand the basic principles behind the phenomena upon which the work is based, this need for complexity vanishes and the redundancies can be eliminated. The work may now exist in its purest form.

Non-Linearity as a Conceptualization in Music

Pozzi Escot

I

It dawns: nothing has been more basic to, nor dominated European thought more than the concept of line.

line is causal
line is fundamental
line is generic
line is infinite
line is primary

Line set the boundaries for the linguistic systems, the formal structures in the arts, the sense of time, the scientific experience. Line operated as the relentless source of connecting threads of functional unity. Line was equivalent to overriding logic.

The first postulates of Euclidean geometry concern the nature of straight lines. Plato's Timeaus (the great astronomer) resolves the dimensions which govern the nature of the universe in terms of causality. The classical mechanics formulated by Galileo and Newton works along the lines of motion and energy - bodies tend to preserve themselves in their straight line unless compelled to change that state by forces impressed thereon.

Centuries of European intellectual and historical development have been based on linear discourse - progression from point to point; furthermore, from small (primeval) to greater (better). Anthropologist Edmund Carpenter notes that the format of the book medium, for instance, favored linear expression, for the argument ran like a thread from cover to cover. Anthropologist Dorothy Lee summarized the importance of line by saying that in our culture the line is so basic that we take it for granted as given in reality.

In *The Value of Science*, the French mathematician Henri Poincare writes that we choose rules for ordering our experiences not because they are true but because they are most convenient. In *Science and Nature*, he notes that our mind has adopted the geometry most convenient. Most convenient equals most linear. And he makes it clear that there exist two indispensable and equally valid realms of intellectual pursuit (the linear and the non-linear). In the words of Josiah Royce: "Certain hypotheses are valuable because by experiment they can be verified or refuted. But there is another important class of hypotheses which, though they can neither be confirmed nor disproved, are yet (indispensible to human thought) because they are devices of the understanding whereby we give conceptual unity (linear causality) and an invisible correctedness to certain types of phenomenal facts which come to us in a discrete form and in a confused variety."[1]

In 1953, in an essay in *Scientific American*, French physicist Dr. Philippe Le Corbeiller noted that we were taught only the geometry of Euclid which is one of continuous lines; the early geometry of Phythagoras is one of array of points. Later Euclid was followed by scientists who went deeper into the mathematics and physics of the continuous - calculus, universal gravitation, etc. According to Le Corbeiller, in the last sixty years a new revolution has taken place and everywhere we look we find that what seems to be continuous is really composed of atoms of all kinds. He concludes that placing limitations upon

162

nature runs quite contrary to the traditional tenets of line; we are not yet adjusted to thinking in terms of atoms and quanta.

On June 19, 1911, Wassily Kandinsky wrote to Franz Marc: "Well, I have a new idea...A kind of almanac with reproductions and articles...We will put an Egyptian work beside a small Zeh, a chinese work beside a Rousseau, a folk print beside a Picasso!"[2] And when that almanac's first edition was finally published (1912), edited by Kandinsky and Marc themselves, it included an article by the Russian painter David Burliuk stating some of the most abiding ideals of the almanac:

> In order to understand the works of the artists of today you have to throw the academic   stuff   completely overboard...(Such artists revealed in their new work new principles of beauty.) The newly discovered law of all the artists is nothing but an upstanding tradition whose origin we find in the works of 'barbaric' art...What we first thought to be the 'clumsiness' of Cezanne and the frantic 'handwriting' of Van Gogh is something greater after all: it is the revelation of new truths and new means. And these truths and means are:
>
> 1) the relation of the object to the elements of the plane
>
> 2) the law of displaced construction
>
> 3) the law of free drawing
>
> 4) the application of several viewpoints
>
> 5) the treatment of the plane and its intersections
>
> 6) the equilibrium of perspectives
>
> 7) the law of color dissonance.
>
> These principles are inexhaustible sources

of eternal beauty.[3]

Burliuk was expressing the concept of non-linearity which was then so new in the works of European painters. Painting was one activity whose non-linear pioneering traits can be traced to scientific discovery and awareness of other cultures' non-linear concepts. From 1900 on, the strides of modern physics have been enormous. Already in 1897 Sir Joseph Thomson had discovered that particles in physics tend to drive form into backgrounds with atomism. Concerning atomic structure, the non-linear field theory investigations, and studies of the electrical nature of matter, all bring forth a re-evaluation of linear deductability.

Many aspects of human experience are touched by this re-evaluation. We know now that linear evolution is absurd. Darwin had mentioned, in reference to genealogical interrelationships, his concept of proximity by descendance - namely, an asymmetric relation not reflexive and non-transitive; not a mere logical relation, as the one of inclusion, suffering to construct linear hierarchies.

Also around this time, contemporary systems of communications began to have, as their premise, non-linearity. The printed media, film and later radio and television, all composed their linguistic communication-beamings on the mere juxtaposition of unrelated material where no single linear strand was to connect the contents. Thus, literature and film were to develop techniques of multiple viewpoints and flashbacks. A multiplicity which stops and questions the linear unfolding of action and events. Authors like Beckett, E. E. Cummings, Ionesco, Jarry, Joyce, Katherine Mansfield, Anais Nin, Pirandello, C. Pozzi, G. Strand, Virginia Wolff, at one time or another, in all or some of their works, throughout these last 100 years, remake literature.

It was Erwin Schrodinger who exposed entropy as a

fundamental condition of the physical world commenting on the natural tendency of things to approach the chaotic state unless averted. This conclusion together with the uncertainty principle of Heisenberg (conveying as a basic postulate of quantum mechanics, that it is impossible to precisely measure the momentum of a particle at the same time as a measurement of its position is made, for particles are not ruled by the laws of causality) and Goedel's proof against the axiomatic method in mathematics (proving that deductability and logical proof are untenable) are significant achievements which finally point to a valid conceptualization of non-linear phenomena.

Line as a primal organizing concept had to be questioned; we were confronted by:

1) atoms and quanta
2) color field creating design and structure
3) differential calculus
4) entropy
5) field and mass concepts and relationships
6) geodesic lines
7) light, reflection as modeling techniques
8) linear ambiguity
9) multi-directional phenomena
10) self-sufficient parts (centripetality)

Linearity as an artistic and scientific conceptualization had been, and is still, recognized through:

1) adjacency
2) causality
3) congruency
4) connected segmentation
5) correlated quantitative precision
6) emergence of structure from the potentiality of the primal material

165

7) functional unity

8) semantic closure

9) semantic homogeneity

10) symmetry

Painters were awed at the turn of the century when African masks were suddenly to be seen in Europe. These masks spoke of an abstraction of linear affection. The expressionist poets confounded their contemporaries with their brevity, inertia, and hidden abstractions; both the former and the latter richly expressing non-linearity. "Schwermut" of the expressionist poet August Stramm (1874-1915) is an example of this non-linear affection:

> Schreiten streben
>
> Leben sehnt
>
> Schauern stehen
>
> Blicke suchen
>
> Sterben wächst
>
> Das Kommen
>
> Schreit!
>
> Tief
>
> Stummen
>
> Wir.

Albeit, we are taught and disciplined to write deductively, the axiomatic method of pedagogy obtains emphasis on explicit explanations. Thus, one given proof suffices to sustain a knowledge where a semantic chain of structures exists.

Art in Africa, says American anthropologist Prof. Robert Plant Armstrong, is atomistic: "a (mere) continuum of actional or narrative surface is created by means of a rich density of discrete actions merely contiguous".[4] It was this non-linear principle which first greatly attracted European painters and influenced the development of many trends in twentieth century

European art. Both African art and music have largely been
ignored because their non-linear logic was misunderstood and
depicted (Burliuk notes) as barbaric. African music, which lacks
the semantic homogeneity of European music (before twentieth
century developments) has an outstanding tradition of hidden
proportions, ambiguity of direction, persistent
cross-accentuation, economy of affecting presence (to borrow
from anthropologist Armstrong), self-sufficient phrases,
interruption, inertia. Unlike the tradition of European musical
compositions where linearity was so essential and systems grew
based on the Greek axiomatic method, African music's time and
language concepts have no adjacency, no sequential order, no
modulatory mechanics, no hierarchy of values or functions. Its
order is less loud and discrete.

The music of *Play Song* (Eve Tribe, West Africa) is a vivid
example.[5]

Its non-linearity first observed: cross accentuation of claps and
claps and voice; interruption; the brevity of the four partitions.

Hidden Geometry

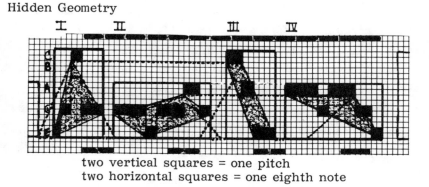

two vertical squares = one pitch
two horizontal squares = one eighth note

167

The non-linear planes:

(lateral superimposition of two seemingly symmetrical planes)

First Plane	Second Plane
registers four and five	register four
tetratonic note collection (F, G, A, C)	tritonal note collection (F, G, A)
disjunct	conjunct
the note collection offers only five intervals, all heard here (in semitones) 0 (3x), 2 (1x), 3 (1x) 4 (1x), 5 (2x)	the note collection offers only two intervals, all heard here (in semitones) 0 (8x), 2 (8x)
soloist	chorus
range = 7	range = 4
total attack points (6 + 6)	total attack points (10 + 10)

seemingly symmetrical planes:

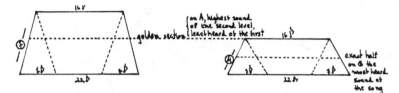

	total duration	total attack-points	total range	units of duration	registral motion
I	11 ♪	6	F4-C5	2x 3x 1x	$\wedge$
II	21 ♪	10	F4-A4	1x 7x 2x	$\vee\!\wedge$
III	11 ♪	6	F4-C5	2x 3x 1x	$\diagdown$
IV	21 ♪	10	F4-A4	1x 7x 2x	$\vee\!\wedge\diagdown$

symmetrical illusion: four interrupted non-generic

partitions, merely contiguous

	tetratonic collection	start-end	polarity	intervals	hidden geometry
I	F (1♪) G (6♪) A (0♪) C (2♪)	F-G	G	0 (1x) 2 (1x) 3 (0x) 4 (0x) 5 (2x)	acute angled scalene triangle
II	F (2) G (13) A (3)	G-G	G	0 (4x) 2 (4x)	four- sided polygon
III	F (4) A (2) C (3)	C-F	C A F	0 (2x) 3 (1x) 4 (1x)	trapezoid
IV	F (2) G (5) A (11)	A-F	A	0 (4x) 2 (4x)	obtuse angled scalene triangle

non-linear characteristics: not one partition sounds the entire note collection

II

In *Science and Human Values*, Jacob Bronowski writes: "the discoveries of science, (and) the works of art are (both) explorations...(and) explosions, of a hidden likeness."[6] The French mathematician Jacques Hadamard talks of the creative process as one of,

> preparation
>
> incubation
>
> correction

The English physicist-mathematician H. E. Huntly writes about what constitutes the essence of creativity.

> surprise = unexpected encounter
>
> wonder   = unexplored world
>
> curiosity = a craving to understand

Jung in the development of his theory of the collective unconscious writes of the secret of effective art: "...who speaks with primordial images speaks with a thousand tongues."[7]

169

Is the creative effort and its result accomplished through entropy-principle-tendency, a struggle towards geometrical order, or a fusion of both an intuitive and mathematical mind? Is it not correct to absorb the fact, without question, that structure is movable in reference to function? Thus, cultures or periods might have similar ingredients fostering the creative effort, but these ingredients can be expressed in entirely different structures without at all lessening the power of these ingredients or the final structure. The Eve song could be perceived to be as beautiful as a Schubert lied. It is known that, in physics, the behavior of atoms arranged in a three-dimensional molecule can be altered drastically if they are removed from that shape. Both songs, after all, have autonomous structural rules.

What logic must govern the world of creativity?

European music for centuries was regarded in terms of melodies, lines really. When these are not conveniently heard, audition fails to understand, and follow, the sonic experience. Melodies - sonic strands - were forced into clear levels of perceptibility through their construction.

1) Each successive frequency in the strand must follow the rule of linguistic logic according to the laws of a given system.

2) Each successive note in the strand must clearly continue to enunciate the dominant spectra over any other accompanying sound.

3) Each successive pitch in the strand must originate from congruent sources and must be sounded by instruments, when different instruments collaborate in its formation, with equal sonic sources.

4) Each successive tone in the strand must continue to prolong the strand to a goal

170

and final assertion.

Theorists have often continued to extend previous theories of linear music beyond their boundaries and encompassing to try to explain the pseudo-melodies of 20th century music and the non-linear musics of other cultures, thus only increasing the malady. Perhaps one can ask if Bach was purely linear; or, in what respect he was linear. Might it not have been obscured that Bach was continuously multilinear; his linear logic overwhelming, but the multiplicity of his melodic lines at times incongruous with each other. This is also the case with the contemporary Hungarian composer Gyorgy Ligeti, especially in his composition for the harpsichord, Continuum (1962), except over two centuries later the melodic lines have disappeared and the precise logic of the tonal system (Bach's system), with its hierarchy of values and functions, is gone.

Gyorgy Ligeti refers to his overall compositional technique with one word: überdeckungseffekte. In the 204 units of Continuum, each consisting of a constant 16 total-attack-points, different sets of additive numbers regulate the linear multiplicity and dynamic symmetry of the work. The cross relationships of the set elements show what, in terms of time activity, is being thrown into forceful sonic relief.

```
10---15--------25------40------65------105----------170
  17--20-------37------57-----94-----------151
   18-----30------48------78-------126----------204
    21----34------55------89--------144
```

Unit

1 = The piece opens with two note patterns for two manuals each sounding G4-Bb4 in contrary motion and intervals 3 - (3) (indicating, respectively, both the horizontal and vertical forms of the

171

interval).

10 = Third pitch sounded,F4, and intervals 2 - (2) and 5 - (5) with a three-against-two note pattern.

15 = Fourth pitch sounded, G#4, and interval 1 with a three-against three note pattern.

17 = Interval (1) sounded with a four-against-three note pattern.

18 = First element of the Golden Section set where the fifth and sixth pitches are sounded, A4 and B4, the interval 6 with a five-against-four note pattern.

20 = End of Bb4 as upper boundary, F#4 as the seventh pitch sounded and interval 4 heard for the first time.

21 = First element of the Fibonacci set, interval (6) sounded with a five-against-five note pattern.

25 = Simultaneous sounding of interval 6 outlining five note patterns.

30 = Return to five-against-four patterns, initiating a gradual decrease of note-pattern contents.

34 = The first unison for both manuals, F#4.

37 = Five note patterns sounded chromatically and in canon.

40 = Return to five-against-three note patterns.

48 = Return to two-against-three note patterns (units 46 to 49). 55 = Section I ends as it began with two note patterns in contrary motion; last unit of the closest

registral space (such reduced range is only heard again in unit 182, Section IV); Section I is essentially characterized by narrow intervals and contrary-motion note patterns; eighth pitch, D#4, is sounded on the very first attack of the next unit 56.

57 = Ending the note-against-note pattern as the lower manual begins a new "arabesque" motion (already felt in unit 56).

78 = The negative Golden Section; G4 sounded again after being dropped at unit 43; a dense unit presenting nine different pitches for the first time.

89 = Section II ends having reached the widest register yet, B3 - D#5, and filling in that range with the sounding of the 12th pitch D completing the chromatic collection; this pitch (D5) is heard for the first time in unit 86, and pitches nine, ten, eleven (C#4, C5, E4) at units 67, 68 and 72; D continues to sound for two units more; intervals 7 - (7) sound in unit 86; the 7, F#4-B3, continues to sound as an ostinato for eleven units initiating the completion of all intervals in their narrow and complementary forms not wider that an octave; at this unit an extraordinary 13 leap links the D4 to D#5; finally, the units around 89 serve as an interlude to Section III, the climactic area.

94 = Last unit of both manuals with a two note pattern, Section III having returned to note patterns.

to note patterns.

105 = gesture initiating the first significant ascending and descending motion of the work. Intervals 8 and 10 present; intervals 9 and 11 have been heard at units 103 and 108.

126 = A magic number in quantum theory and the unit of the positive Golden Section; a register explosion takes place (16' + 8' = 4'); the 12 interval is heard completing, at last, the intervallic series; tritones outline the three note patterns of both manuals; this registral explosion initiating a yet wider and deeper ascending and descending motion. 144 = Section III ends, one manual dropping the 16' + 8'; Section IV opens with a sustained three note simultaneity.

151 = For three units 150 - 152, only one manual is struck, sounding a 3.

170 = Final unit of four-against-three note pattern as the lower manual soars up a final time in diminishing density.

204 = Last unit of the work, E7 concluding a symmetric sonic framework.

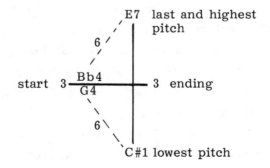

E7 last and highest pitch

6

start 3 Bb4/G4 ──── 3 ending

6

C#1 lowest pitch

III

Dr. Abraham Moles, the French psychologist, refers to musical perception (in relation to information theory) as a musical message which is broadcast in a succession of packages of originality of varying size. The closer we come to the music of the 20th century the more differentiated, the more non-linear, these successive packages can be. One marvel of non-linearity is Anton Webern's Drei Kleine Stucke opus 11 for cello and piano of 1914. The first movement is here analyzed.

1) Ambiguity

Bipartite Division (54 ♪)

♩=58	rit.	♪=58	accel.	rit.	♩=58	rit.	♩=58
12♩	3♪	3♩	6♩	3♪	6♩	3♪	18♪

A   B

Tripartite Division (54 ♪)

♩=58	rit.	♩=58	accel.	rit.	♩=58	rit.	♩=58
12♩	3♪	3♪	6♩	3♪	6♩	3♪	18♩

a   b   c

Bipartite division:

- each part has four small partitions
- each part has a total of thirty-three pitches
- each part has a total of twenty-seven eighth notes

175

- each part has eighteen and a half eighth notes of total attack-sound duration
- each part has eight and a half eighth notes of total silent duration
- each part has two "a tempo" indications (eighth note = 58) and begins "a tempo"
- each part has four chords.
- each part has eight different pitches for the cello.
- each part begins and ends with a silence.
- each part begins with two equal total-attack-points.
- each part has the same tritone sounding for its four partitions, (D-G#, G-C#, C-F#, E-Bb).
- each part's four small partitions have ranges adding up to 139,

1) F#2-G#5	= 38	5)	B2-Bb5	= 35
2) E2-Eb6	= 47	6)	Eb2-Ab4	= 29
3) G#2-F#4	= 22	7)	G2-F#6	= 47
4) F2-C#5	= 32	8)	Bb2-D5	= 28

$$\overline{139} \qquad\qquad \overline{139}$$

- each part has the same number of pitches for registers 2, 5 and 6, while 3 and 4 balance each other,

Registers	2	3	4	5	6
Part a	6	9 + 12		5	1
Part b	6	10 + 11		5	1

- each part balancing the lowest and highest pitches of the cello and piano, F#2-F#6 and Eb2-Eb6,

176

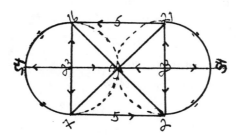

Tripartite division:

a) "a tempo" to "rit."

   begins silent

   ends with a sound

   has two partitions

   piano has thirteen notes

   has a range of 47

   has two chords

   has eight total attacks

   lasts for fifteen eighth notes

b) "a tempo" to "rit."

   begins silent

   ends with a sound

   has four partitions

   piano has twenty-three notes

   has a range of 43

   has three chords

   has eighteen total attacks

   lasts for twenty-one eighth notes

c) "a tempo"

   begins silent

   ends silent

   has two partitions

   piano has thirteen notes

   has a range of   47

   has three chords

   has ten total attacks

   lasts for eighteen eighth notes.

2) Hidden Proportions

1--2--3--5--8---13-------21-----34--55
3---6--9-12-15--18-21-27-33--54

Fibonacci series sounding significant musical events:

-one eighth note, silence
-two eighth notes, silence
-three eighth notes, the work opens with cello's lowest note
-five eighth notes, silence
-eight eighth notes, piano sounds its highest note alone
-thirteen eighth notes, the first ritenuto
-twenty-one eighth notes, the negative Golden Section initiating the climax (based upon the proportion of .382-1, since the positive is .618)
-thirty-four eighth notes, the last ritenuto (at thirty-three eighths, the positive Golden Section, the piano sounding the lowest note of the work, Eb2 followed immediately by F#2, the same note with which the cello begins the composition)
-fifty-five eighth notes, the work lasts fifty-four eighth notes; one instance of ritenuto, however, at thirty-four, is not balanced adding the extra duration.

Multiples of three dividing the work into a succession of packages of originality of varying size:

-three eighth notes for the fifth small partition
-six eighth notes for the first, third, fourth, sixth and seventh small partitions
-nine for the second small and third large partitions
-twelve eighth notes for the last small and second large partitions
-fifteen eighth notes for the first large partition and first part of the tri-partite division
-eighteen eighth notes for the last large partition and last part of the tri-partite division
-twenty-one eighth notes for the second part of the tri-partite division
-twenty-seven eighth notes for each bi-partite division
-fifty-four eighth notes for the entire composition.

The four large partitions are characterized by the following:

- each begins "a tempo" and ends "rit." on the last 3 eighth notes (the last one ends "a tempo")
- each has a note distribution of sixteen, seventeen, fifteen and eighteen, in that

order

- each partition is separated by a silence
- the first two alter dynamics from ppp to sfp and f at exactly 4.5 before their endings; the last two remain p-ppp
- the first two have complete chromatic collections; the last two have incomplete collections of eleven and ten
- the first two sound their chords on the second total attack point; the last two sound their chords on the first total attack point

```
duration of piece    ┌───────── 54 ─────────┐
bipartite division   ┌────── 27 ─┐ ┌── 27────┐
tripartite division  ┌─15┐ ┌──── 21 ──┐ ┌─18┐
large partitions     ┌─15┐ ┌─12┐ ┌─9 ┐ ┌─18┐
small partitions      6  9  6  6  3  6  6  12
```

3) Entropy, as Understood in Information Theory, with the Coefficient Eight (a Fibonacci Number)

- eight small partitions
- eight chords
- eight different total note durations
- eight different pitches in the cello for each bipartite division
- eight velocity changes
- eight different dynamics
- eight as the interval of the smallest partition's lowest and highest pitches from

piece's corresponding boundaries;

Eight small partitions:

1) Presents two total attacks in the middle of its six eighth note duration; the cello sounds its lowest pitch F#2, the piano an arpeggiated chord in the highest register of all chords; the partition sounds only ppp and contrasts stasis and motion.

2) Presents six total attacks beginning with silence and ending with sound; the cello sounds a sfp harmonic, B5, which drops an expanded 23 to a Bb3; the piano combines stasis and motion - the previous chord shifting register and permuting the pitches minus the D and the horizontal activity sounding the 1-3-6 cell beginning with the highest pitch Eb6 of the piano; the first "rit." at the last three eighth notes; the partition sounds ppp-pp except for the sfp.

3) Presents a re-enactment of partition one - the piano shifting to the F#2 of the cello to register four then sounding a chord followed by the cello's three attacks with an irregular up-bowed near-the-bridge motion; the "a tempo" speeds up, and the partition ends and begins with a silence; sounds ppp-pp.

4) Presents outstanding aspects; continues the speeding up for three eighth notes before abruptly changing to three eighth notes "rit."; the negative Golden Section

on its very first attack - a six-note chord rich in tritone sound; the dramatic 3 of the cello intensely articulated and noisy; the falling 6 of the piano; the only dotted-eighth-sixteenth-eighth activity for three eighth notes of the piece's total rhythmic flow; the only partition to start on a sound attack; four different total attack durations mostly in register four (the most heard pitches in this register of any partition); f for the partition.

5) Presents yet another metamorphosis of the first partition; lasting only three eighth notes it sounds two total attack points; the piano overtaking the previous 3 of the cello in the subdued and quieter register five; the partition whose sonic boundaries lie equidistantly from the respective limits of the entire piece; sounds pp. a dynamic which will pervade until the end.

6) Presents its linguistic gesture - the 1-3-6 cell - as if distributed in space and time; the cello sounds two extreme timbres; the piano's first two attacks sound the lowest pitch of the piece immediately followed by F#2, the lowest pitch of the cello; the positive Golden Section occurs at this moment, the two significant pitches initiating an upward motion of almost two octaves; the last "rit." ends this partition which, in total, has the most attack points.

7) Presents its musical gestures as if

stagnated; three attacks sound two chords and the cello's highest pitch F#6 as an overtone; still another seeming first partition.

8) Presents the longest small partition; cello sounds the most attacks with a complete 1-3-6 cell "sul ponticello"; the piano sounds its longest duration ending with the narrowest range of any chord.

Eight chords (x = new pitches; o = repeated pitches):

	1	2	3	4	5	6	7	8
F#3								x
Eb4							x	
G2							x	
C#45				x	o			
Bb23				x		o		o
B2				x		o		
C35			x		o			
G#35	x	o			o			
E2345	x	o		o			o	
A234	x	o		o	o	o		o
F234	x	o	o	o				
D45	x		o		o	o		

the small partitions

(partition six has no chord)

184

In the bipartite divisions ending with the widest and narrowest chords, 31 and 11, not one interval is common to all of the chords; the first bipartite division opens and ends with all-interval chords which are more dense. As the chromatic collection is completed, density lessens.

Eight different durations:

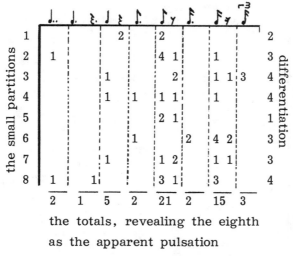

the totals, revealing the eighth
as the apparent pulsation
1, 2, 3, 5, 21 = Fibonacci
1+2+2+2+3+5 = 15

185

Eight different pitches in the cello:

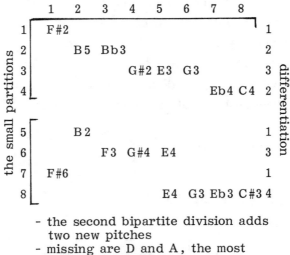

	1	2	3	4	5	6	7	8	
1	F#2								1
2		B5	Bb3						2
3				G#2	E3	G3			3
4							Eb4	C4	2
5		B2							1
6				F3	G#4	E4			3
7	F#6								1
8						E4	G3	Eb3	C#3 4

the small partitions / differentiation

- the second bipartite division adds
  two new pitches
- missing are D and A, the most
  heard in the piano

Total number of pitches (x = cello; o =
piano):

	reg. 2	reg. 3	reg. 4	reg. 5	reg. 6	Totals
B	2o 1x			1x		4
C		1o	1x	2o		4
D		2o	3o	2o		7
E	o	1o 1x	1o 2x	1o		7
G#	1x	2o	1o 1x	1o		6
G	1o	1o 2x	1o	1o		6
A#	1o	2o 1x	1o	1o		6
A	1o	1o	4o			6
C#		1x	3o	1o		5
D#	1o	1x	1o 1x		1o	5
F	1o	2o 1x	1o			5
F#	1o 1x	1o	1o		1x	5
	12	20	22	10	2	66

B, C: 11; D, E: 11 — 22

G#, G, A#, A, C#, D#: 11, 11, 11, 11 — 44

(2, 10, 12, 22 = additive numbers)
49 piano pitches; 17 cello pitches

186

Eight dynamics:

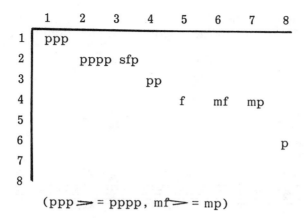

	1	2	3	4	5	6	7	8
1	ppp							
2		pppp	sfp					
3				pp				
4					f	mf	mp	
5								
6								p
7								
8								

(ppp $\Longrightarrow$ = pppp, mf $\Longrightarrow$ = mp)

Eight as the interval of the smallest partition's lowest and highest pitches from the piece's corresponding boundaries:

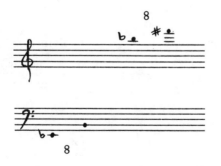

187

4) Apparent Linearity and Causality

Tritone cell in the eight small partitions:

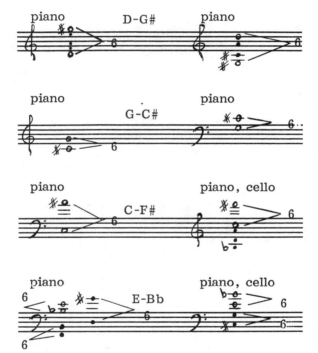

The linguistic cell 1-3-6:

small partitions:

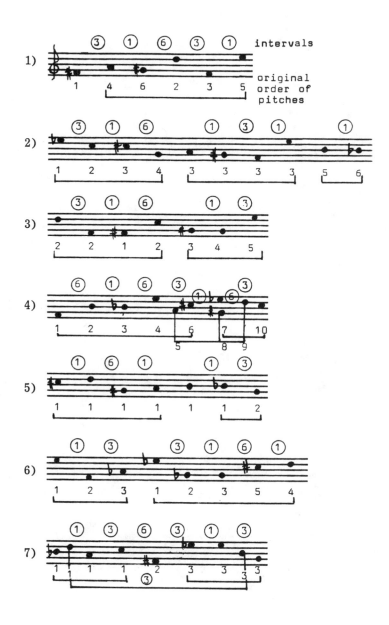

8)

1) James R. Newman, editor, *The World of Laws and the World of Chance* (New York: Simon and Schuster, 1956), p. 1378.

2) Wassily Kandinsky and Franz Marc, editors, *The Blaue Reiter Almanac* (New York: The Viking Press, 1974), pp. 15 - 16.

3) *Ibid.*, pp. 78 - 80.

4) Robert Plant Armstrong, *Wellspring* (Berkeley, California: University of California Press, 1975), p. 62.

5) A. M. Jones, *Studies in African Music*, Volume II (London: Oxford University Press, 1959), p. 2.

6) Jacob Bronowski, *Science and Human Values* (Harmondsworth, England: Penguin Books, Ltd., 1958), p. 9.

7) C. G. Jung, *Man and His Symbols* (Reading, Massachusetts: Addison-Wesley, Inc., 1964), p. 89.

On Political Texts and New Music

Christian Wolff

The renewed, and new, political awareness emerging in the later 1960's in the United States and parts of Europe was apparent also in a variety of music - folk and popular (drawing on an older, sometimes submerged, tradition), jazz (long associated with the struggles of blacks), and avant-garde. The association of elements of the latter with progressive politics had its precedent too, for example, in the work of Hanns Eisler in the late twenties, of the American composers of the Composer's Collective in the thirties,[1] and of Luigi Nono starting in the fifties. By the late sixties and early seventies a number of younger composers of the avant-garde began to associate their music explicitly with political preoccupations. Among these (the list is not exhaustive) were Cornelius Cardew and Dave Smith in England. Erhard Grosskopf and Nicolaus Huber in Germany (Hans Werner Henze, though in a somewhat older generation and a more eclectic tradition of composing, might also be mentioned), Louis Andriessen and Peter Schat in Holland, Yuji Takahashi from Japan, and Garrett List, Fredric Rzewski and myself in the United States. All these composers support some form of democratic socialism. (As far as I know, no composer associated with the post World War II avant-garde has made an explicit connection of his music with a conservative political position.) John Cage's influential work is a special case. Although he has maintained firmly that music must have no "propaganda" function, he nevertheless represents, in both his music and his

193

writings, an individualist-anarchist position close to the tradition of Thoreau.[2]

The ways in which music and political content can be associated are of course various, and the questions raised by such an association are many. Here I will only attempt to give an account of some of my own work, primarily in the musical setting of texts with an explicit political content, and to consider some of the questions I have found raised by it.

Two general sets of questions are on the horizon of the works which I will discuss. The first has to do with the "literary" aspect of the works, or, more generally, the sense in which they may be formalized as cultural products. For the most part the texts set to music are not as such "literary", not poems or plays. They are documentary, taken from letters, interviews, speeches, manifestos and the like (this is also the case with a number of the works by the composers mentioned above.)[3] Their original intent is direct political statement. The use of such texts for musical setting of course formalizes them in a new way. In practical terms, the formalization inherent in the context of their presentation may be very different - the difference, for example, between a speech delivered to a politically concerned group and the same speech set to music and performed for a concert audience. A crucial point here, by which to gauge the degree and kind of this difference, is the class character of the politically concerned group and of the concert audience. If the group and audience are close in class interest, the difference in formalization may not matter very much. Another practical factor will be the purpose, or the occasion, of the speech and of the speech-set-to-music, whether, for instance, there is a specifically hortative intention or a more generally commemorative one. Very generally, we are dealing here with the familiar point that music, being non-verbal, will inevitably have some formalizing effect on any verbal material associated with it; but then, this formalization in turn may well intensify the expressive content of the combination of text and music, may in fact cause a new "content" or meaning to appear.

It is worth mentioning that the questions raised by the musical setting of non-literary texts have some affinity with those raised by the "documentary" literature which began appearing in the late 1960's, e.g. plays of Rolf Hochhuth and Peter Weiss.

The second general set of questions related to the pieces I will discuss has to do with the music's connection to the avant-garde.[4] The main issue here is the compatibility of the situation of new music with progressive political content. Two polar positions can be exemplified: the one by Cornelius Cardew, who insights that there can be no politically effective avant-garde art and rejects his own earlier (and distinguished) work in experimental music in favor of musical styles related either to a folk and popular tradition or to the most expressive elements of nineteenth-century art music; and the other by Luigi Nono, a long time member and important functionary in the organization of the Italian communist party, who composes in an uncompromisingly advanced manner, making full use of serial techniques and electronics. The difficulties raised by the avant-garde context are, principally, of three kinds. One is the drive towards extreme individualism, the compulsion to be different in one's work, so that an "advanced" position is staked out. The results may be a wasteful competitiveness; the risk of one's work being turned into a novelty product for commercial advantage; or the risk of being isolated. Another, familiar problem inherent in the avant-garde is its tendency to esotericism or ivory-towerism which makes impossible the wider communication necessary for political content. To be sure, these difficulties are symptomatic of a disordered cultural situation; and, if they are embraced consciously, may serve to concentrate a critical attack on that cultural situation.[5] Another potentially positive feature of avant-garde work is its encouragement to technical experimentation and a continuing development of formal and technical resources. But one last question remains. For whom is the cultural work being done? What, for example, will be a musician's position before a politically progressive audience, or simply a working class audience, whose cultural experience has largely been determined by commercial "popular" art?

In the late 1960's, trying to find ways of providing new music for non-professional performers, including people with no previous practical musical experience, I made a set of pieces consisting only of brief prose instructions.[6] There was no need to be able to read musical notation. The instructions were the scores, characterized by a combination of precise specifications and general, suggestive guidance so as to enable the performers both to focus their playing and yet to play freely. I intended a kind of exploratory improvisation, free of specialized virtuosity and of the technical and psychological pressures associated with concert performance. I also hoped to bring about among the players a feeling for self-imposed discipline as well as individual freedom, both in turn made possible, and given resonance, by their need to work together.

Making these pieces I found myself dealing very directly with primary musical materials and resources, for example, with any person's capacity to produce a rhythmically articulated sound with any means available, including the parts of one's body, and any person's capacity to use his or her voice musically. The pieces thus include four songs. The texts are brief: "crazy mad love"; a name, to be chosen by the singer (variable therefore from performance to performance); "no more beer" together with "fee fie fo fum"; "you blew it." Generally, the texts are used as sound material, usually with some accompanying instrumental material. They are broken down into syllables and phonemes or just single letters from which the voice must make a sound. These elements are variously repeated, like pitches in a scale or the timbres of a set of instruments. Here is one example (the complete song):

"Crazy Mad Love"
Number of articulations (of any kind) per word, using any of the three title words, in any sequence and freely repeated: 5 2 1 2 11 2 1 3 3 1 2. "1" articulation must be managed as far as possible, particularly with the two syllable word; observe the numbers in the sequence given, which can be repeated as often as desired and cut off at any point: spaces, pauses between numbers (articulations of single words) are free.

The same numbers and requirements apply to each non-vocal production of a sound. Include at least one vocal and one non-vocal playing in any performance.

From one to six people can play.

Because the texts are short and their elements repeated, though fragmented, their sense still emerges. For performance the texts, on the one hand, when fragmented, provide sound material (including, in the above example, a specific guide for non-vocal sounds; on the other hand, the texts' semantic content and expressive suggestiveness give direction to the particular shaping of the sound material. The origins of the texts are casual and personal: a half-remembered phrase from a rock-'n-roll song, an exchange between a child and his uncle; "you blew it" was a sudden, angry response to a Nixon speech on Vietnam war policy. But these personal associations are not indicated in the music; the words of the texts are let go, so to speak, for the performers to find and make their own associations from them. Each text has its range of expressive possibilities which may be variously chosen and individualized (re-individualized, in fact).

These pieces contain no overt political statement. Yet, the way they function (which, incidentally, is partly made possible by the fact that the "scores" are themselves verbal instructions rather than traditional symbolic notations) could be seen to have political implications. The requirement of cooperative, more or less leaderless performance and its flexible conditions suggest a kind of democratic libertarianism and the spirit of some of the movements of alternate, communal social life characteristic of the late sixties (this was not my conscious intention, but I was interested in and sympathetic to the ideas of these movements at that time). In retrospect, however, though positive in a number of ways, the communal movements were essentially apolitical, that is, they set out to practice social alternatives without any coherent plan for changing society as a whole, and therefore, in the end, would be compelled to depend on it. This illusory self-sufficiency, a kind of utopianism, must also be said to characterize these compositions. Their political weakness lies in a disregard of the audience, of a potential representation of larger social elements. To put it another way, the hope implied in the music, that the audience will want to become performers themselves, that the music, because technically accessible to performance by any one willing to try, could thus function educationally - this hope seems to have an inadequate basis. The difficulty can also be seen in a technical consideration: the lack of guidance in the music for rhythmic articulation. This vagueness about rhythm tends to cause an inward, contemplative and "time-less" feeling in the sound production, and to inhibit an outward projection of sound which could extend a sense of energy instead of enclosing it. In fact, the music is most liable to break away from this tendency to self-enclosure through the song texts. Finally, though, these texts too have their limitations, mostly in being so brief. Repeated, as said, they become intelligible (semantically, linguistically). But extended repetition can also neutralize their individual force, making them more and more like "meaningless" incantation.

My next attempt at setting a text was in a solo piano piece in which the pianist must also speak or sing, *Accompaniments*, written in 1972 for the composer and pianist Fredric Rzewski.[7] The piece is in four parts; the first sets the text, the remainder, partly with accompanying percussion also played by the pianist, is a kind of musical aftermath of the text, a commentary on it and a sound landscape through which it can resonate. The text, taken from Jan Myrdal and Gun Kessele's *China: The Revolution Continued* (New York, 1970), consists of remarks transcribed by them of a veterinarian and a midwife in the village of Liu Ling in the Yenan area of northwest China. The speakers describe the development of their work as it was affected by the Cultural Revolution. I chose the text because of its immediacy - the sense of the speakers' presence and their direct way of talking; and because of their clear political awareness. They describe and illustrate how ordinary, daily problems, having to do with sanitation and contraception, are dealt with from a consciously political point of view. Free of rhetoric or abstract dogma, a sense of progress through political and educational struggle is conveyed with matter-of-fact good humor and optimism.

This is how the text is set. Units of lengths varying from one to sixteen syllables are marked off; sometimes a unit will coincide with a semantic continuity, sometimes not. Here, for example, is a sequence of nine units:

Not everyone looks after their latrines pro-
-perly. Dry earth
must be
used for covering them. There must be no flies.
We have got quite a long way with
our hygienic work, but not the whole way.
That is why unremitting pro-
-paganda is needed against
the bad old habits.

For each unit there is a sequence of sixteen (and sometimes thirty-two; a sequence plus its transposition) four-note chords, each chord different but related harmonically to the others in the sequence. The pianist speaks or sings the text, accompanying each of its syllables with one of the chords (melisma is excluded). The pianist is free (a) in the ways he or she projects the text, that is, whether by speaking or by any kinds of singing; (b) in the choice of pitches, if singing (i.e. no pitches are specified for the text); (c) in the choice of chords from a sequence, so long as no chord is repeated: (d) in the rhythm or spacing of the chords; (e) in the number of repetitions of a unit of text which has eight or fewer syllables, so long as no more than sixteen chords, each different, are used (thus, in the example above, the first, fourth, sixth and eighth units cannot be repeated, while the second could be repeated up to three times, the third up to seven times, the fifth and seventh once, and the ninth twice; no repetitions, however, are obligatory, and hence not all chords in a sequence will necessarily be played); and finally, (f) the pianist is free to make a selection of units from the text as a whole - since the text is long and a complete presentation of it would not be appropriate in most performing situations. Instructions also specify that the choices made, though variable and flexible, should allow a coherent sense of the text to emerge. The text thus serves as a guide to performance, both in detail and as a whole. It requires of the performer full attention to its meaning before it can be used (in this respect it is like the prose instructions which made up the pieces described previously).

The performer must function in two ways, one professional and specialized, as pianist, the other non-professional - a way shared with any number of people, speaker or singer. The latter requires readjustment of the notion of professionalism and is intended to overcome some of the isolating features of a specialized activity. These two ways correspond here respectively to music and text (the text would be far more widely accessible to performance than the music). The interchange implied between the two ways in which the performer must work is also represented in what actually happens when the text and music are performed together. On the other hand, the rhythm of the text, the way one speaks its language, tends to affect the rhythm of the accompanying chords. Though the player may choose, as he is free to do, to impose on the text's language independent rhythmic shapes, the text, because of its longer and explicit continuities of statement, will keep reasserting its own rhythm. On the other hand, the pitch at which the text might be sung, which is free of any explicit specification, will tend to be drawn into relation with the (given) pitch configurations of the accompanying chords.

Why, then, has the text been set in this way? As indicated, for the performer; so that there is something to grapple with which will require both reflection and independent choice. (One could almost say that a process of education is suggested for the performer, which she or he will exemplify, reflecting the education described in the text.) The composition itself formalizes an every-day, documentary text which is politically illustrative: in order to publicize it (the text in its

201

book communicates only to the individual reader), to return it to public speech in new situations, and, with the music, to give it expressive force. (For myself, incidentally, it was also a matter of discovering the poetry in this apparently ordinary, prosaic material - and attempting to publicize that.)

More particularly, breaking up the text into phrases by a syllable count and matching each syllable to a chord was intended to express a certain sobriety and discipline, and ground the vocal expression in a certain austerity (hence the absence of melisma). The chords were made to give the music a full, resonant sound; to articulate a musical structure, like a pattern of stanzas, with which the text must mesh; and, by their harmonic logic, to represent a disciplined, forward movement (like the one described by the text). Each individual sixteen-chord sequence (corresponding to the individual line of a stanza) consists of all the ways one four-note chord can be read if, when the chord is written on one stave, the notes in the chord are read in all the possible combinations produced by referring each note to either treble or bass clef. This always results in sixteen chords which generate one another harmonically in such a way that, as the sequence proceeds, a logic of development is also generated, and the sequence has the effect of an extended cadence which ends not on a point of return, as in functional harmony, but as a new, yet logically necessary conclusion. The music begins with thirty different sequences - the first section (or stanza); these are then repeated, with some shifting in their order - a second section; thirty sequences of thirty-two chords each follow, each sequence a combination of one of the first thirty and its transposition a major third higher - a third section; and, finally, the last section consists of fifteen sequences from those which had been transposed up in the previous section. Of course, unless the player chooses to use all the material (the exceptional case), this structure will not be completely represented in any one performance: it is an available scaffolding.

Unlike the earlier prose pieces, the first part of *Accompaniments* sets a text with a clearly political content, of some length; and, because professional (and solo) performance is involved, it is far more detailed and demanding in its musical scoring. Further, the scoring is such that a sound of some strength and rhythmic movement is assured; the music as a whole will have an extroverted character. But the music and the treatment of the text, as well as the range of freedom left to the performer, are still "experimental." There are risks entailed. Partly, I think, these are valuable. For instance, they require of the performer a clear committment and a special alertness, and may have a similar effect on an audience. However, it is still the case that the experimental character of the setting of the text may appear, to certain audiences, simply eccentric, and worse, may make the text itself seem to be ridiculous. It may be that there is too great a strain, or contradiction, between this kind of text and the way it has been formalized.

The last piece I will discuss represents, among other things, an attempt to delimit the range of contradiction between text and setting.

Wobbly Music is a piece for mixed chorus and a group of instruments (piano or electric piano, guitar, two melody instruments, as available; others may be used as well).[8] It was written in 1974-75 for a student and community group directed by Neely Bruce at Wesleyan University in Middletown Connecticut. It is a longer piece (about thirty-five minutes), made up of a series of "numbers" (eight altogether), like a cantata. The texts relate to the history and principles of the I.W.W., the Industrial Workers of the World, more familiarly known as "Wobblies," the most progressive and revolutionary force of large scope in the labor movement in the United States.

203

It was also a movement distinguished by its tradition of militant and humorous songs.[9]

The first three numbers of the piece are songs from this tradition: "Bread and Roses," written during the celebrated, and successful, strike in the mills at Lawrence, Massachusetts in 1912, a beautiful song expressing the determination and aspirations of the women whose role in the strike had been decisive (it has been revived by the women's movement of the 1960's); "John Golden and the Lawrence Strike," a song, using an older hymn tune ("A Little Talk with Jesus"), with text by the Wobblies' most famous song writer, Joe Hill, describing some of the specific circumstances of the strike, in particular, the mill owners' attempt to neutralize the Wobbly-led strikers through accomodating leaders of the established unions (John Golden - "he'll settle any strike if there is a coin in sight" - is their agent); and "The Preacher and the Slave," also known as "Pie in the Sky," again set to an older hymn, a sentimental favorite of the Salvation Army ("Sweet Bye and Bye"), with new words by Joe Hill which are a devastating parody of the original text's soothing promises of a better life in the distant here-after.[10]

After these three songs there is an instrumental interlude, a kind of overture to the four numbers which follow (and an interval in which the singers rest). The first of these sets the text of the Preamble to the I.W.W. constitution of 1908, the general principles of the movement. Next comes a new setting of the text of the second song, "John Golden and the Lawrence Strike"; a setting of an excerpt from a speech made by Arturo Giovannitti, one of the main strike leaders, who had been framed on a charge of murder in order to have him out of the way, "If there was any violence"; and the closing number, "It was a wonderful strike," which sets an excerpt from a speech by Bill Haywood, the Wobblies' most prominent national leader, summarizing the significance and main achievements of the Lawrence strike after its successful conclusion.

The songs and text settings are for the whole singing group. There are no solos and no distribution of parts by the usual soprano, alto, tenor and bass categories. The basis of the singing is unison or heterophonic; all pitches are given in treble clef, each voice to sing in its comfortable octave. In two of the numbers the melodic lines, sometimes single, sometimes in two parts, are made up of units of a few notes (mostly from one to three) passed back and forth between subdivisions of the chorus (up to four subdivisions, each including representatives from the various voice ranges). This makes a kind of counterpoint in space as the sound moves from group to group of singers, and allows the subgroups' individuality to emerge while requiring the whole chorus' shared effort of coordination to produce the sum of the text and music. In this way too the text can be more clearly articulated and intelligible - which would be impossible with the usual counterpoint of vertically simultaneous lines. The text is not represented simply by one homogeneous mass of voice: you are meant to hear individualized voices and the drama of the voices' helping one another to carry the meaning on.

The text guides the music closely because, in this case, it has both a clarity and comprehensiveness of statement which I thought required as direct a setting as possible. Its semantic movement, through phrase, sentence and paragraph, instigated, in detail, the note rhythms, and determined, overall, the music's structural articulations. (There is occasional melisma, but usually to make the rhythmic adjustment between text and music easier.) The pitch organization of the music is drawn from the first three songs, whose tunes are associated with the political movement which the texts represent. The pitches of these tunes are set up as scales (interval sequences) which then undergo a series of transformations (various kinds of transposition) that move them, as it were, forward harmonically (as in *Accompaniments*, the harmonic procedure is not self-enclosed, with return to a tonic, but evolutionary). (One exception to this procedure is the

205

number "If there was any violence." There the pitch material is mostly confined to the instrumental accompaniment, while the voices speak or declaim without specific pitch. This material is extracted from the accompanying instrument - guitar - itself: chord sequences derived from the instrument's tuning, here specially altered. The guitar of course would have been the typical accompanying instrument of the older songs: and the altered tuning allows the basic, open string resonance to represent the typical accompanying chords of triad and diminished seventh.) *Wobbly Music*, then, sets its text and draws the musical material (pitches) of that setting from the music originally associated with the text. This at least, through a kind of historical cross-referencing, makes for a closer coordination of the text and its formalization.

The choice of text material for the individual numbers suggested the arrangement of the order of the numbers; that is, the structure of the whole piece, which is, in turn, expressed by the music. "Bread and Roses," because it has again become familiar, though with different, yet related, political associations, is the opening number; it links its original sense with the present. It is connected to the eighth and last number, "It was a wonderful strike." The latter takes from it its pitch material and carries forward its feeling of confident affirmation and the expression of a need for continued, united struggle. This last number also uses, for the first time in the piece, percussion, played by the singers (as well as chosen by them), to give a final, sharp edge of sound. As noted, the text of the second song, "John Golden and the Lawrence Strike," is used again with new music, whose pitch material is derived from the original song's music, in the sixth number. "The Preacher and the Slave," the third number, provides pitch material for the setting of the Preamble, the fifth number. These two texts are among the best known which represent the Wobblies in general - they are the only ones in the piece which do not relate

206

specifically to the Lawrence strike. The instrumental interlude, the fourth number (which was written last), is made up of material drawn from each of the subsequent numbers. Only the seventh number, "If there was any violence," stands somewhat apart (though some of its musical material is used in the instrumental interlude). Its text, which both relates to the events at Lawrence and transcends them as a statement of principles, is the strongest and most impassioned in the piece, and, as said, is set without singing pitches. This overall structure, then, has correspondences and symmetries: the fourth number relates to the fifth, sixth, seventh and eighth; the third to the fifth; the second to the sixth; and, framing the whole, the first to the eighth. These are intended to show the interconnection of the piece's parts and to suggest a cumulative force in their progression.

Compared to the pieces described earlier, *Wobbly Music* is the most explicit in its notation. The score can still be used flexibly, to accomodate available performers and allow choices of interpretation, but the range of flexibility is narrower. This is due partly to the larger number of performers involved, whose coordination needs more initial guidance, and partly to the clarity and unambiguous force of the text. Like the earlier pieces, it has a didactic element, for the performers - through the texts they sing and through the musical conditions under which they sing[11] - and, potentially, for the audience. In the previous pieces the relation of the music to its audience is the most unpredictable element of all. Unless composers and performers can take over complete responsibility for the conditions of individual performances, this unpredictability, under present social and cultural circumstances, will necessarily continue. In *Wobbly Music* there is, by the inclusion of traditional material in the three opening songs, an initial effort to find, or at least inform, an audience. It could also be said that the larger number of performers, making up a community of their own, become an audience too, or rather, they can begin to represent the breaking up of a sharp division between audience and performers. This is one direction in experimental music which can support a politically progressive position.

The use, in *Wobbly Music*, of older music is not intended as an exercise in nostalgia; nor of course is the use of older political texts. In each case, music and text, it is a matter of "using the past to serve the present." It may, for example, be useful to recall some of the basic sources of the socialist argument - as plainly stated at the opening of the Preamble: "the working class and the employing class have nothing in common"; or as Giovannitti said at his trial (the conclusion of the seventh number): "I say you cannot be half free and half slave, and economically all the working class in the United States are as much slaves now as the negroes were forty or fifty years ago; because the man that owns the tools wherewith another man works, the man that owns the house where this man lives, the man that owns the factory where this man wants to go to work - that man owns and controls the bread that that man eats and therefore controls his mind, his body, his heart and his soul." As for the older music, it is also important to recall the tradition of popular political music of which it is a part, a tradition notably neglected by the mass media (and by most formal music education). That it should be a popular music also affects the new music drawn out of it. It stands as a model for non-subjective writing, avoidance of eccentricity, economy and directness of expression, accessibility to a wide range of participants, humor (in the use of rhythm and timing) and militancy (again, in rhythmic procedures, and in the sound qualities of the accompanying instruments). A number of these features are close to aspects of experimental music, particularly where it is concerned with the subordination of individualistic self-expression, accessibility to a range of performers, and economy of technical means. What the new music contributes is

208

principally additional means for achieving these ends; a spirit of practical freedom from conventional compositional models (not necessarily to eliminate them, but simply to find, without formal prejudice, what works best with these texts); and a distinctive new sound. The newness of the music should be a mark of vitality, signaling what is now to the point in the older texts.

1) Cf. R. S. Denisoff, *Great Day Coming: Folk Music and the American Left* (New York: Penguin, 1973), pp. 38ff.

2) See, for example, his collection of writings *M* (Middletown, Connecticut: Wesleyan University Press, 1973). A discussion of Cage's use of language in musical composition and its political implications would be of great interest, but is beyond the scope of these notes.

3) For earlier examples one might cite Hans Eisler's *Zeitungausschnitte* and Luigi Nono's *Il Canto Sospeso*, whose texts are taken from letters of prisoners of war written during World War II.

4) The term "avant-garde," so far used very broadly, might have been distinguished from "experimental." Leading representatives of the former I take to be such continental European composers as Boulez and Stockhausen, while the latter, "experimental music," seems initially and principally an American and English phenomenon whose central figure is John Cage. See Michael Nyman, *Experimental Music: Cage and Beyond* (New York: Schirmer Books, 1974); cf. also, in the context of an extended discussion of the notion of "avant-garde," M. Calinexcu, *Faces of Modernity* (Bloomington, Indiana: Indiana University Press, 1978), pp. 144 - 145. A general, critical view of the new music movement as a whole, during the 1960's and 1970's can be found in E. Fubini, *Musica e Linguaggio Nel' Estetica Contemporanea* Torino: Piccola Biblioteca Einaudi, 1973), pp. 116 - 133. Composers of music with explicit political content, however, come from both camps, avant-garde and experimental.

5) Cf. J. Habermas, *Legitimation Crisis*, translated by T. McCarthy (London: Heinemann, 1976).

6) *Prose Collection, Experimental Music Catalogue* (London: 1970 and 1974) and in G. Quasha, ed., *An Active Anthology* (Freemont, Michigan: 1974), pp. 123 - 126.

7) The music is available from C. F. Peters (New York), and has recently been recorded by Rzewski on CRI S-357. Rzewski had recently written a particularly impressive piece for instrumental ensemble with a speaker - *Coming Together* (recorded on Opus One 20). Occasionally he would perform this piece himself as a solo, playing the instrumental material on the piano and speaking the text as well - a remarkable feat, because the music and speaking run, without pause, in a fairly rapid, unbroken rhythm for nearly twenty-five minutes. It was this performance which suggested to me asking the pianist both to play on the keyboard and at the same time to use his voice. A critical discussion, from a political perspective, of both *Accompaniments* and *Coming Together* can be found in Cornelius Cardew, *Stockhausen Serves Imperialism* (London: 1974), pp. 64

- 67.

8) Available from C. F. Peters, N.Y.

9) A good collection of material from and about the Wobblies can be found in J. K. Kornbluh, *Rebel Voices: An I. W. W. Anthology* (Ann Arbor, Michigan: University of Michigan Press, 1964). See also M. Dubofsky, *We Shall Be All: A History of the Industrial Workers of the World* (New York: Quadrangle Books, 1974). The texts used in *Wobbly Music* can be found in Kornbluh and *The Autobiography of Big Bill Haywood* (New York: 1929, reprinted in 1974).

10) Texts and music of these songs in E. Fowke and J. Glazer, ed., *Songs of Work and Protest* (New York: Dover Books, 1973) and B. Stavis and F. Harmon, eds., *Songs of Joe Hill* (New York: Oak Publications, 1955).

11) In this respect the piece is like Brecht's *Lehrstucke*.

Contributors

Robert Cogan (b. 1930; Detroit, Michigan) is widely acclaimed as both a composer and theorist. He studied at the University of Michigan and Princeton University, and has received numerous awards including a Fulbright Scholarship and a Guggenheim Fellowship. He is co-author of *Sonic Design: The Nature of Sound and Music*, one of the most important theoretical treatises to have appeared in recent years. As a theorist, Robert Cogan is responsible for an important body of research into the nature of tone color, research which has had a profound impact on the development of his own composition. His music has been recorded on Gold Crest, Spectrum and Delos. Robert Cogan is presently Chairman of the Department of Graduate Theoretical Studies at the New England Conservatory of Music.

Thomas DeLio (b. 1951; Bronx, N.Y.) is a noted composer and theorist. He studied at the New England Conservatory of Music and Brown University where he received a Ph.D. in an interdisciplinary studies program combining mathematics, music and the visual arts. His articles on these subjects have appeared in *The Musical Quarterly*, *Perspectives of New Music*, *The Journal of Music Theory*, *Artforum* and *Interface*. As a composer, Thomas DeLio has distinguished himself in the area of computer aided composition and as the creator of a series of live electronic sound installations. His music is published by Dorn Publications and recorded on the Spectrum label. Thomas DeLio has taught at Clark University and The New England Conservatory, and is currently a member of the faculty of the Department of Music of the University of Maryland at College Park.

Pozzi Escot (b. 1933; Lima, Peru), a composer and theorist, was educated in both Europe and the United States. She is the co-author of *Sonic Design: The Nature of Sound and Music*, one of the most important theoretical treatises to have appeared in recent years. As a theorist, Pozzi Escot has explored the notion of non-linearity in both contemporary music and world music, and has published several papers on this important subject. As a composer, she has created an exciting body of music, the structural basis of which is derived from mathematical group theory and topology. Her works are published by Publications Contact International and are recorded on both Delos and Spectrum. Pozzi Escot is currently on the faculty of the Music Department of Wheaton College in Norton Massachusetts.

Alvin Lucier (b. 1931; Nashua, New Hampshire) is a major figure in contemporary American music. He studied at Yale University and did graduate work at Brandeis where he also taught and directed a chorus noted for its performances of new music. Through his own compositions, he has demonstrated an extraordinary understanding of the diverse physical properties of sound. In addition, his unique approach to composition has challenged many basic attitudes concerning the roles of both the composer and perceiver in, respectively, the creation and appreciation of a work of art. Alvin Lucier's works have been heard and widely acclaimed throughout Europe and the United States. A complete collection of his scores appears in *Chambers*, a book of interviews with Douglas Simon published by Wesleyan University Press. Recordings of his major compositions are available on Lovely Music/Vital Records. Alvin Lucier is currently Chairman of the Department of Music at Wesleyan University in Middletown, Connecticut.

Christian Wolff (b. 1934; Nice, France) is an internationally renowned composer. He received a Ph.D. from Harvard University in comparative literature, a subject which he has taught, in addition to music, at several notable institutions.

Though largely self-taught in composition, he has written numerous articles on contemporary music for such periodicals as *Die Reihe*, *Collage*, *Audience* and *Sonus*. As a composer Christian Wolff has distinguished himself as the creator of a unique approach to indeterminacy in which performer interactions are given priority over all other compositional parameters. Since the early '70's he has been involved with contemporary political issues. In works of this period, he has attempted to project the basic principles of a political ideology known as democratic socialism through compatible musical structures. Christian Wolff is currently a member of the faculty of the Music Department at Dartmouth College in Hanover, New Hampshire.

Wesley York (b. 1949; Portland, Maine) is a composer, theorist and artist. He studied music, literature and the visual arts at Clark University, and composition at the New England Conservatory of Music. His analytical work with the music of such contemporary composers as Philip Glass constitutes a remarkable exploration into the nature of structure and perception. In addition, as a result of his expertise in both the aural and visual media, he has evolved a rather unique approach to both instrumental and electronic composition which has recently extended into the area of computer music. Wesley York is also a highly respected visual artist currently working in the Boston area.